CONTENTS

INTRODUCTION

THE BEST OF
INDIAN
COOKING

Photography by Ashley Barber

Published by Bay Books
61–69 Anzac Parade, Kensington
NSW 2033, Australia.

© Bay Books

Some of the recipes included in this book have been reprinted
from *The Commonsense Indian Cookery Book* by Sara Matthews,
with the permission of Angus & Robertson Publishers.

National Library of Australia
Card Number and ISBN 0 85835 756 9

Acknowledgements
The publishers would like to thank Josiah
Wedgwood & Sons (Australia) of Sydney, and Verna
and Beverley Pearson for their assistance during the
preparation of this publication.

This book is intended for those who enjoy Indian-style food and would like to learn to cook it for themselves, their family and friends. It covers a wide range of basic recipes and cooking methods, as well as providing serving suggestions and recipes for traditional accompaniments. The entertaining section (p. 9) gives ideas for cooling drinks to serve with hot curries, and guidelines for Indian-style dinner parties.

Wherever possible, curry recipes have been listed with a hot, medium or mild rating.

All the ingredients used are readily available in supermarkets, grocery stores and shops specialising in spices or Eastern foods, and the instructions are given in simple, step-by-step form.

It is not necessary to buy a wide range of exotic ingredients (which will perhaps be used only occasionally) to make the recipes in this book. The spices and ingredients on page 7 that are marked with an asterisk (*) are those used most often. Once these are at hand, you will be able to complete most of the recipes in the book.

Alternatives have been suggested for spices and foods which you may not have. If no alternative is mentioned in the recipe itself, check through Basic Ingredients (on the following pages) where possible substitutions are listed after the description of each foodstuff. Substitutions will not always give the same flavour to a dish as the original ingredients, but they will go part of the way towards it. (An exception is the substitution of evaporated milk for cream of coconut. Obviously these flavours are not similar. The alternative is intended for people who do not like the taste of coconut. The evaporated milk balances the recipe and gives a creamy effect without a strong coconut flavour.)

For many people who are just beginning to cook Indian dishes, the idea of working with strange spices can seem rather daunting. But in fact a few of the spices will be quite familiar — cloves and cinnamon, for example, and perhaps chilli, paprika and ginger. The interested cook will soon learn to recognise and work confidently with cumin, coriander, turmeric, cardamom and the rest.

Spices should be as fresh as possible. It has been assumed in the recipes that most spices are to be used in powder form. They can be bought by weight at health-food stores and shops which specialise in Indian foods, or, more expensively, in jars and packets in supermarkets and grocery stores. If you intend to use the spices infrequently, buy only a small quantity at a time. Keep spices in tightly capped jars to keep them fresh.

When using spices, remember that they need to be cooked to produce their rich, distinctive flavours. It is unwise to add extra spices at the end of the cooking, in order to change or correct the taste of the dish. The spices will taste 'raw' and will conflict with the tastes of the cooked spices.

Indian dishes and ingredients

Basic Ingredients

Ingredients listed below that are commonly used are marked with an asterisk (*), and together form a good basic store of Indian spices and foods; the Indian terms are given in brackets.

Black pepper* (*kali mirch*)   may be bought as small, black peppercorns and used whole or freshly ground, or as powder.

Bay leaves   dried leaves of the bay laurel tree, used in flavouring many foods. Substitute a small sprig of coriander leaves for 1 bay leaf. Note: substitution will alter flavour.

Besan   often known as lentil flour — low in gluten and high in protein. If not available, use the following substitute. Roast yellow split peas in a heavy saucepan, being careful to turn constantly so as to prevent burning. Cool, then grind in an electric mixer or food processor as finely as possible. Put through a fine sieve and then store in a tightly covered jar.

Cardamom* (*illaichi*)   an important curry spice, strong and aromatic, available as pods and powder. Substitute 2 cardamom pods, crushed, for ¼ teaspoon of powder.

Chilli* (*mirchi*)   available as fresh, green chillies, dried red chillies, chilli powder, and chilli paste. Chilli gives colour, flavour and heat to most Indian-style dishes. Those who are not used to hot foods should use only a little chilli at first, and gradually increase the quantity as desired. Chilli can also be omitted entirely — the recipes will work quite well without it, though will not taste quite so exotic. Substitute 1 small capsicum for 2 green chillies, or 2 tablespoons chilli paste for 2 tablespoons chilli powder.

Chilli sauce*   a hot sauce useful as a dip for meat balls and other savouries; may be used in place of chilli paste in an emergency. Substitute tabasco sauce or tomato sauce as a dip. Note: flavours are different.

Cinnamon* (*dalchini*)   available as bark (cinnamon stick) or powder; an important curry spice, aromatic, warm and sweet in taste. Substitute 15 mm of cinnamon stick, crushed, for ¼ teaspoon of cinnamon powder.

Cloves* (*laungi*)   available whole or powdered; an important curry spice, strongly aromatic and pungent.

Commonly used spices and flavourings

Coconut cream* (*narial*)   concentrated coconut available in many supermarkets and shops specialising in Indian foodstuffs, often in the refrigerated section. Used as is or dissolved in water. Store in refrigerator. Substitute, for liquid coconut cream, an equal quantity of canned coconut milk or evaporated milk. Note: evaporated milk substitution will change the flavour of the dish.

Coconut milk   available in cans or may be made by dissolving coconut cream in water, 30 g–60 g coconut cream to every ½ cup water, depending on thickness required. Substitute, for every ½ cup coconut milk, plain evaporated milk or ½ cup evaporated milk in which 30 g–60 g desiccated coconut has been soaked and strained out. Note: substitutions will change the flavour of the dish. A useful blender method for making coconut milk is to add 250 g desiccated coconut to 600 mL warm water. Place ingredients into blender and blend to a smooth puree. Squeeze through muslin over a basin to remove the first milk. Repeat this process for second milk adding same amount of water again to the original coconut. This will freeze very well or can be kept in a refrigerator. The rich cream will rise to the top of the milk and can be spooned off and used separately.

Coconut, desiccated   dried grated coconut, used in some curries and Indian desserts, for making coconut milk, some chutneys, and salads.

Coriander* (*dhania*)   used extensively in seed and powder form — this gentle, fragrant spice is an important curry ingredient which rounds and balances the hotter spices. Coriander leaves are often used as a garnish in Indian cooking and as an ingredient in salads, chutneys and some curries. Coriander is easily grown in a pot. It is also known as Chinese parsley. Substitute for powder an equal quantity of curry powder; for fresh leaves, use celery leaves.

Cumin* (*jheera*)   an important curry ingredient with a warm, aromatic taste. Available in powder form.

Curry powder   blended curry spices. Mixture may be mild or hot according to recipe. Commercial curry powders to not give the flavour of a home-made curry mixture.

Curry paste   a paste made of blended curry spices, generally more expensive but giving superior results to the commercial curry powders.

Fenugreek   seeds used whole or ground in curries. Strong aroma and slightly bitter taste. Use in small quantities.

Garam masala* a strongly perfumed mixture of several spices, often added at the end of cooking. May be bought already mixed where spices are sold, or made at home by following either of the following recipes.

20 g cardamom seeds
20 g cinnamon stick
7 g black cumin seed
3 pinches mace
3 pinches nutmeg powder
Grind the first four ingredients together to make a smooth powder. Add nutmeg. Mix and store in airtight jar.

125 g coriander seeds
30 g cinnamon
60 g peppercorns
½ teaspoon nutmeg powder
60 g cumin seeds
30 g cloves
60 g large cardamoms

Roast the coriander and cumin seeds separately. Peel the cardamoms. Grind all the spices and store in an airtight container.

Garlic* (*lehsun*) a pungent bulb which separates into cloves; it is peeled, crushed, pounded or chopped to add flavour to all types of food.

Ginger* (*adrak*) the root of a tropical plant, available fresh, powdered and canned. Preserved, sugared ginger is used as a sweetmeat. Recipes in this book specify fresh ginger, which should be scraped before being pounded or shredded. Vary the amount of ginger used to suit your taste. Substitute ¼ teaspoon ginger powder for 1 thin slice of fresh ginger.

Ghee the clarified butter in which Indian food is traditionally cooked. Substitute, as a cooking medium, cooking oil, butter or margarine; in bread and dessert making, use butter or margarine.

Lemon grass a fragrant herb which may be bought in dried form or easily grown in the garden.

Lime juice fresh juice of the lime — a member of the citrus family. Substitute for 1 tablespoon lime juice, 1 tablespoon vinegar mixed with one teaspoon sugar; or use equal quantity fresh lemon juice.

Mint a refreshing, tangy herb used in salads and chutneys, as a curry ingredient and as a garnish. Easy to grow in pot or garden; also available in dried form.

Mustard seed (*sarson*) used whole or crushed in curries; has a strong, hot flavour and is generally used in small quantities.

Nutmeg (*jaiphal*) a pungent spice, available whole or in powder form.

Onion* (*peeaz*) sliced or chopped onion, fried golden brown, is used as the base for most curries. The frying caramelises the sugar in the onion and releases the delicious flavour and aroma. Onion rings, fried or raw, are commonly used as a garnish, and onion is also used extensively in salads.

Pappadums paper-thin lentil cakes which may be bought in packets at supermarkets and specialty stores. When fried in hot oil they swell, curl and double their size.

Rice* (*chawal*) brown and white, served with curry or as a base for dishes such as pilaus and birianis. See Rice chapter for further information.

Semolina (*sujee*) grain commonly used to make puddings and sweets.

Sesame oil a fragrant oil obtained from the sesame seed. Use in very small quantities.

Soy sauce made from soy beans, very extensively used in Chinese cooking as ingredient and condiment.

Tamarind pulp from the pod of the tamarind tree, used in making tamarind water, a common curry ingredient. To make tamarind water, soak a piece of tamarind (about a tablespoon) in ½ cup hot water and allow to stand for 15 minutes. Strain water into another container, squeezing tamarind pulp as dry as possible. Discard pulp. Use more tamarind pulp if a stronger taste is required. Substitute for ½ cup tamarind water, 1½ tablespoons tamarind paste or 2 tablespoons lime or lemon juice; or use ½ cup vinegar.

Tamarind paste* (*imli*) a convenient method of adding tamarind to curry, used alone or mixed with water to make tamarind water. Substitute for 1 tablespoon tamarind paste: 6 tablespoons tamarind water; or 1½ tablespoons lime or lemon juice; or 3 tablespoons vinegar. If a stronger, sour taste is required then more tamarind can be used.

Turmeric* (*haldi*) a golden-yellow fragrant spice extensively used to colour and flavour curries, vegetables, rice and savouries. Saffron is an adequate substitute.

Yoghurt* (*dahi*) milk curd, used in its natural form both as a curry ingredient and a curry accompaniment — plain, spiced or with cucumber.

Note: When using liquids and needing to convert cup

and spoon quantities to metric equivalents, use the following measures.
1 cup = 250 mL
1 tablespoon = 20 mL
1 teaspoon = 5 mL

Entertaining

An Indian dinner party usually consists of several main dishes (meat, fish and chicken), one or two vegetable dishes, salads, bread, rice, pappadums, several chutneys and pickles. The dishes are placed in the centre of the table, and the guests help themselves. This serving method, and the fact that most of the dishes can be eaten with a fork, make Indian food very suitable for a buffet meal or a large party.

Serving suggestions   Here are a few points to remember when choosing dishes to serve:
- Not everyone likes, or can eat, very hot, spicy food. So serve dishes, chutneys and pickles of varying degrees of 'heat'.
- Serve a balance of dry and moist dishes for variety.
- Pappadums and yoghurt may be served with any combination of dishes.
- If you wish to serve bread, but do not wish to make your own, any crusty, uncut loaf will substitute. Serve warm.
- Serve plenty to drink with the meal — cold water, fruit juices, soft drinks, or cold beer. Wine may also be served, although some people may find that it does not combine well with hot, spicy curries.
- Indian dinner parties should be informal. Guests may serve themselves and eat with their hands.
- Break bread with your hands. Keep generous quantities of paper serviettes handy. Alternatively, supply small bowls of warm water with a slice of lemon for the 'washing of finger tips', in traditional Indian style. One of these bowls follows each course in India where most eating is done by hand.

Refreshing drinks   For a refreshing curry accompaniment try the following drink recipes. In both recipes the quantities of the ingredients have been calculated to make one 800 mL serving, sufficient for a large jug.

LASSI (Buttermilk)
320 mL natural yoghurt
4 tablespoons sugar, increase according to taste (caster dissolves faster)
400 mL water
salt (optional — add to taste)
1 tablespoon of rose water essence, or increase according to taste (check concentration of rose water used)
ice cubes
mint leaves (optional)

Blend until frothy in a blender or food processor. Float a few mint leaves on top if preferred. As an alternative to this sweet version, you may prefer to substitute a teaspoon of salt and a ¼ teaspoon of black pepper for the sugar.

NIMBOO PANI (Fresh lime juice)
2 cups fresh lime or lemon juice
640 mL water
3 tablespoons sugar, or to taste
salt (optional — add to taste)
mint or rose petals (to taste)
crushed ice

Mix ingredients together until sugar dissolves. Gently crush the mint or rose petals by hand to release the aroma and add them to mixture. Serve with ice and a twist of lemon. If you want to add 'punch', a nip of vodka or gin will do very nicely.

BREADS

Unleavened breads are a universal, daily staple. The Indian version is called *chapati* and resembles a Mexican tortilla in appearance. It has many variations: chapati refers to the light, thin variety, while the thick type is called *roti*.

There are also many other forms of bread which can be fried or baked. *Pooris* are deep fried — they puff up and become very light. *Parathas* are shallow fried and are heavier — they can be served either plain or stuffed.

All dishes except dessert are eaten with bread and rice. Bread and rice, however, are eaten at different stages of a meal, and which is eaten first depends on the prevailing custom. Where rice is a delicacy it is usually eaten first.

All forms of Indian bread should be served hot. Most can be prepared a little earlier and reheated in a conventional oven or microwave. Any bread that is fried should be allowed to drain on paper towels. Seal breads in foil after cooking — they remain fresh longer. If reheating in a conventional oven, seal bread in foil.

Pappadums

These are pancake-like wafers made from lentil flour. When dropped into hot oil for a few seconds they more than double in size and become very crisp. They can be served with all types of curry. Pappadums can be purchased in packets and should be stored in an airtight tin.

Chapatis

3 cups fine wholemeal flour (attah)
1½ teaspoons salt
1 tablespoon ghee
1 cup lukewarm water

Place flour and salt in a bowl.
Rub in ghee.
Add water and mix into a firm dough.
Knead dough 10-15 minutes until elastic.
Cover and rest for 1 hour.
Pinch off pieces of dough about the size of a large walnut and roll out on a lightly floured board into a thin circle.
Heat griddle or heavy frying pan, place one chapati at a time on griddle and leave for 1 minute.
Turn and cook the other side.

Indian breads

Press lightly around edges of chapati to encourage bread to rise a little.
Place cooked chapatis on a plate and cover until all are ready.
Serve immediately with butter to accompany dry curries or other dishes.
Makes 6-8 chapatis.

Plain Flour Chapatis

375 g plain flour
2 teaspoons salt
140 g butter
cold water as needed
60 g melted butter

Sift the flour and salt together into a bowl and add 45 g butter cut in small pieces.
Blend in with pastry blender till mixture is consistency of bread crumbs.
Now add just enough cold water to knead into a soft dough.
Divide into 8 parts.
Take one part of the dough and roll out round like a small plate.
Brush with melted butter, dust with flour and roll up into a ball again.
Do this twice more.
Now roll each ball into a flat chapati.
Heat the griddle to white heat and put the chapatis on it one at a time.
Bake 1 minute each side.
Brush round the edges with melted butter and fry, turning, till both sides are brown and crisp.
Lower the flame under the griddle once the frying starts.
See that the griddle is white hot for each new chapati.
Makes 8.

Vegetable Chapatis

315 g wheat flour
1 teaspoon salt
1 onion
1 tablespoon coriander or watercress leaves
½ capsicum
30 g cooking fat
cold water

Sieve the flour and salt together.
Slice the peeled onion thinly. Mince the capsicum and coriander.
Mix the onion, minced leaves and capsicum well together with the flour and salt.

Add as much ice-cold water as required to make a soft dough.
Divide up into walnut sized balls.
Flatten and roll out to the sized of a cheese plate.
Heat the griddle to white heat, brush it with cooking fat and fry the chapatis (they should be like thick pancakes) on both sides till brown in colour.
Makes 6-8.

Stuffed Parathas

125g wheat flour
1 small horseradish
1 teaspoon salt
60g butter
cold water

Sieve the flour and salt together.
Blend in 15g butter and make into a soft dough with cold water.
Divide into 8 parts.
Grate the horseradish.
Roll out each of the 8 pieces thinly to a round shape.
Spread the horseradish on one round and cover with another.
Make four stuffed parathas all together.
Heat the griddle white hot and fry in rest of butter.
Lower flame and cook gently.
All kinds of mashed, boiled or grated vegetables can be used instead of horseradish.
Makes 4.

Rogni Roti

500g wholemeal flour
3 tablespoons cream
salt to taste
150mL milk
60g ghee

Sieve flour and add the salt, cream, ghee and milk.
Knead the dough till soft and pliable.
Make balls the size of a large egg and roll into rounds the size of a small plate.
Cook on a very hot griddle, like chapati.
Makes 24.

Poori
(Deep Fried Bread)

500g plain or wholemeal flour, sifted
120g ghee
cold water

Knead flour with water to make a soft pliable dough.
Keep covered with a damp cloth for an hour or so.
Knead again till the dough is smooth and does not stick to the hands.
Make small balls the size of an egg.
Roll these out on a floured board till they are the size of a small saucer.
Heat the fat in deep frying pan till smoking and put in one poori at a time.
With a flat spoon or spatula, press the poori gently till it puffs out; turn and cook till pale golden.
Drain and keep hot or serve at once.
Makes 24.

Semolina Pooris

250g flour
125g semolina (sujee)
½ teaspoon turmeric
1½ teaspoons salt
30g rice flour
45g butter
30g fat for frying
cold water

Mix the flour, semolina, turmeric and salt.
Add 30g butter in little pieces and blend with a pastry blender till it is like sand.
Form into a soft dough with cold water, kneading the dough well.
Now add 15g butter to the rice flour and beat with a rotary beater till creamy.
Roll out the soft dough into a large circle and spread the rice flour mixture evenly on it.
Roll it up and roll out again.
Cut into largish rounds with a biscuit cutter and fry in the heated fat in the frying pan.
Use oil or butter as liked, but the fat must be hot.
As soon as the cut rounds are put in they must puff up.
Serve at once, before they subside.
Makes 24-30.

Coconut Bread

2 tablespoons desiccated coconut
1 teaspoon salt
3 tablespoons wheat flour
pinch cayenne pepper
¼ teaspoon sugar
60g cooking fat

Mix all the ingredients together and form into a soft dough with cold water.
Roll out into small flat cakes.

Dosa with Potato Stuffing

Fry a few at a time in the heated cooking fat in a frying pan till cooked and lightish brown.
Makes 6-8.

Dosa

Eaten extensively in southern India, dosa originated among the poorer people who were, in the main, vegetarians.

185 g rice flour
185 g plain flour
a little chilli (optional)
2 tablespoons yoghurt
salt to taste
1 tablespoon ghee

Mix the rice flour with the plain flour.
Add salt, yoghurt, ghee and water and make into a thick batter.
Keep overnight to ferment, not in refrigerator.
Cook in a pan spread thinly like an omelette.

Serve hot with vegetables (see following recipe) or meat curry.

Potato Stuffing for Dosa

250 g potatoes
¼ teaspoon turmeric
¼ teaspoon chilli
30 g ghee
1 medium onion
¼ teaspoon mustard seeds
salt and pepper

Boil the potatoes.
Peel and dice.
Chop the onion finely.
Heat the ghee and fry the mustard seeds.
Add the onions and fry till half done.
Add potatoes, turmeric, chilli and salt.
Cook for 5 minutes till dry.
Add pepper.
Put a spoonful of this mixture in each dosa and serve.

RICE

Rice is served at every meal in India and is an ideal accompaniment to curries of all types. It also forms the basis of dishes such as *pilaus* and *birhianis*.

The many different varieties of rice fall into three basic categories: round grain rice (the least known), short grain rice (used mainly for desserts) and long grain rice (fried or boiled — used as a base for most of the dishes in this book).

The best long grain rice is *basmati*, a delicious, aromatic variety which is easy to cook well. It is not stocked everywhere, but specialist shops will certainly be able to supply it.

Brown or natural rice is unpolished and must be cooked in a greater quantity of water and for longer than polished rice. It has a superb nutty flavour, and is firmer in texture than white rice.

Well cooked rice is fluffy and dry, and every grain is separate. It should not be sticky and mushy — sure signs of overcooking and too much stirring. To test whether rice is cooked, rub a grain or two between finger and thumb. If the grains are soft, with no granules, the rice is cooked. Wash rice thoroughly before and after cooking to remove excess starch.

To reheat the rice use any of the methods described below.

- Place in a colander over a pan of simmering water, and cover. Stir occasionally with a fork until all rice is hot.
- Place in a buttered, ovenproof dish. Cover with buttered greaseproof paper (butter-side down) and a lid. Bake in a slow to moderate oven, 120°C–175°C (250°F–350°F), for 15 to 20 minutes.
- Place in a saucepan, add a little water and steam over low heat, covered, for about 5 minutes or until warmed through. Stir with fork or chopstick and remove.
- Heat a little oil in a frying pan, add rice, and stir with a fork over low heat until warmed through.
- A microwave is an ideal, quick and economical way of reheating. Times vary with quantity (usually 2 or 3 minutes on high) so check your instructions booklet.

Cooked rice can also be frozen and reheated when required.

Plain Boiled Rice (White Rice)

Wash 500g rice in cold water four or five times, until water is clear. Add cold water to come 2.5 cm above rice in a saucepan. Bring to the boil, reduce heat to

Saffron rice

medium and continue cooking until water evaporates leaving air bubble holes through rice. Reduce heat to low. Place lid on saucepan and continue cooking for 20 minutes. Do not stir or lift lid during cooking time.

Another method for boiling rice is to add it to a very large pot of rapidly boiling salted water and cook at a rolling boil, uncovered, for 15–20 minutes. Drain in a colander.
Serves 6-8.

Saffron Rice

3 cups long grain rice
3 tablespoons ghee
2 finely sliced onions
1 teaspoon ground turmeric
¼ teaspoon saffron powder
5 cups chicken stock
½ teaspoon peppercorns
¼ cup sultanas
½ cup almonds, sauteed in oil until golden brown
1 cup cooked peas

Wash rice in cold water several times to remove starch and dry with kitchen paper.
Melt ghee in a heavy base frying pan, and saute onion until pale golden.
Add turmeric, saffron and rice and stir well to coat rice with ghee.
Fry until rice grains are just golden (approximately 5 minutes.).
Add boiling stock, salt and spices, stir well, bring to boiling point.
Turn heat very low, cover pan tightly, and cook for 20 minutes.
Do not lift lid or stir during cooking time.
Turn off heat and leave uncovered for 10 minutes to release steam.
Loosen rice grains with a fork, fold in sultanas, almonds and peas.
Goes well with chicken curries.
Serves 4-6.

Tomato Rice

250g rice
2 medium onions
¼ teaspoon garam masala
1 teaspoon salt
60g ghee
1 large tin tomato juice
1 clove garlic
¼ teaspoon ginger
¼ teaspoon chilli

Wash the rice and soak in cold water for an hour.
Slice the onions finely.

Grind the garlic to a paste and mix in the ginger and chilli.
Heat the ghee in a saucepan and fry the onions until golden brown.
Add the garlic paste and garam masala and fry for a few minutes till the masala is cooked.
Put in the strained rice and fry till lightly coloured.
Add the tomato juice, salt and sufficient water to come about 2.5 cm above the rice.
Bring to the boil and cook over low heat till rice is ready, or put into the oven at 175°C (300°F) and when the liquid is nearly dry cover and leave till rice is cooked.
Goes well with Korma Lamb or Beef curries.
Serves 4-6.

Saffron Kedgeree

250g rice
15g currants
15g almonds
60g desiccated coconut
4 medium onions
2½ teaspoons salt
10 cloves
½ teaspoon cumin seeds
120g lentils
8 green chillies
5 dessertspoons sugar
4 threads saffron
½ teaspoon ginger powder
10 cardamoms
4 small sticks cinnamon
180g ghee

Blanch and slice the almonds.
Wash and dry the currants.
Slice the onions thinly.
Soak the coconut in 300mL hot water for 10 minutes, then squeeze out the milk and strain it.
Dry roast the saffron and mix in the coconut milk.
Coarsely grind the cumin and cardamom seeds.
Heat the ghee and fry the almonds and currants till the almonds are medium brown.
Remove and reserve.
Fry the onions till they are crisp and brown.
Wash the rice and the lentils.
In one saucepan put in 150mL water, the rice and 1 teaspoon salt.
Half cook the rice and put into a large pan.
In another saucepan put 75mL water, the lentils and 1 teaspoon salt and cook for 20 minutes or till half done.
Add this to the rice.
Add also ½ teaspoon salt, the saffron mixed with the coconut milk, some of the almonds and currants, fried onions, green chillies (sliced) and all other spices.

Add the sugar and the fat in which the onions were fried.
Mix thoroughly and cover.
Bring to the boil and simmer till rice and lentils are cooked.
Stir the kedgeree with a fork and leave on a very low heat for 5 minutes more.
Remove and serve sprinkled with the rest of the almonds and currants.
Serves 4-6.

Chicken Pilau

500g chicken
600mL yoghurt
45g melted butter
375g rice
2 cloves garlic
2 tablespoons lemon juice
1 tablespoon garam masala
2 tablespoons sugar
1 teaspoon saffron threads
4 medium onions
½ teaspoon ginger powder
1 tablespoon salt.

Wash and drain the rice.
Wash the chicken and cut into large pieces.
Dry fry the saffron, crumble and put into the lemon juice.
Slice the onions and grind the garlic.
Make a paste of the garlic and ginger.
Fry one onion golden brown and remove.
Rub the garlic paste into the chicken and put into a bowl with ¾ tablespoon garam masala, half of the saffron juice, 450mL yoghurt, fried onion, 1½ teaspoons salt.
Mix all together and leave for an hour.
Turn the contents of the bowl into a saucepan and simmer over a very low heat till the chicken is tender.
Take a large saucepan and fill it three-quarters full of water.
Bring to the boil and add the rice.
Cook on a high heat till the rice is nearly ready, drain and put the rice into a bowl with the rest of the yoghurt, ¼ tablespoon garam masala, sliced onions, sugar, melted butter and the rest of the salt.
Mix thoroughly.
Now put half the rice mixture in a saucepan, then the chicken and gravy, the remaining saffron juice and the rest of the rice.
Cover and simmer over a low heat till the rice is cooked, stirring with a fork occasionally.
Serves 4-6.
Serve with vegetable curries and cucumber raitas.

Keema Pilau (p. 18)

16

Vegetable Pilau

250g rice
185g ghee
60g cauliflower
60g potatoes diced
½ teaspoon turmeric
½ teaspoon ginger
2 cardamoms peeled
60g shelled peas
60g sliced carrots
60g French beans, sliced
2 medium onions
1 bay leaf
4 cloves
4 peppercorns
salt to taste
boiling water

Wash vegetables and rice and drain.
Slice onions finely.
Heat the ghee in a large saucepan and fry the onions golden brown.
Remove and keep warm.
Fry the vegetables in the ghee one at a time, and put aside.
Now add the spices and fry till the cloves rise to the surface.
Add the rice and fry for 2 minutes, stirring all the time.
Add 900mL boiling water and boil till the water is nearly all gone.
Turn into a fire-proof dish, add the fried vegetables and put in a slow oven 140°C (275°F) for 15–20 minutes.
The dish should be covered when put in the oven.
Serve with the fried onions sprinkled on top.
Serves 6-8.
Good with fish or prawn curries.

Keema Pilau

500g rice
250g ghee
1 teaspoon ginger
1 teaspoon chilli
1 stick cinnamon
a few strands saffron
500g lean meat, minced
125g finely sliced onions
2 teaspoons coriander
8 cloves
2 tablespoons yoghurt
salt to taste

Fry the onions in the ghee till golden brown.
Add the mince and all the spices except the cloves and cinnamon.

Cook till the mince is nicely browned then add the yoghurt and fry till a rich brown.
Soak the saffron in water and add to the mince.
Add salt, stir and remove from the heat.
Wash and drain the rice.
Put the rice, cloves, cinnamon and 2 teaspoons salt in a large pan.
Add enough water to come 6cm above the level of the rice.
Bring to the boil, cover and simmer till the water has almost evaporated and the rice nearly cooked.
Remove from the heat.
Take a large casserole and put in a layer of rice then a layer of mince and so on till all the mince and rice are used up. The last layer must be rice.
Put on the lid and place in a slow oven for 20 minutes till the rice is cooked.
Before serving mix the pilau very carefully so as not to break the rice grains.
Serves 6-8.
Goes well with vegetable curries, Spiced Yoghurt and Tomato Sambal.

Fish Pilau

1kg fish cutlets (firm-fleshed fish should be used)
500g rice
2 large onions
185g ghee
2 teaspoons chilli
salt to taste
2 teaspoons coriander
2 teaspoons garam masala
1 stick cinnamon
1 large peeled cardamom
6 cloves

Wash and drain the fish.
Slice onions finely and fry them in the ghee till golden brown.
Lower heat and fry the coriander, chilli and fish.
When the fish is brown remove from the heat and keep aside.
Boil 2 litres of water and add the washed and drained rice and the cinnamon, cardamom and cloves tied in muslin.
When the rice is cooked drain in a colander.
In a casserole put a layer of rice, then a layer of fish curry and so on, ending with a layer of rice.
Sprinkle garam masala on the top, cover and cook in a slow oven for 15 to 20 minutes.
Serves 8-10.
Serve with Pumpkin and Mustard Salad.

Vegetable Pilau

Coconut Rice

3 cups good long grain rice, washed and drained
140g coconut cream mixed with 3 cups water or
3 cups canned coconut milk
salt to taste
Garnish: ½ cup raisins, fried until swollen
1 onion, sliced and fried golden brown
6 tablespoons slivered almonds, lightly fried

Put rice, coconut cream, water and salt in a saucepan.
Bring to the boil on medium heat, and boil until
liquid dries up.
Reduce heat, cover, and continue cooking until rice
is well cooked and fluffy. Gently stir with a fork.
Garnish with fried raisins, onion and almonds.
Serve with Kofta Curry and Cucumber and Pineapple
salad.
Serves 4-6.

Fried Rice (With Ham and Eggs)

2 tablespoons cooking oil
2 cloves garlic, chopped finely
1 small onion, chopped
2 eggs, beaten
salt and pepper
½ teaspoon sesame oil
1 teaspoon soy sauce
125g ham, cut into strips
4 cups cooked rice
125g cashew nuts, fried

Heat oil in a pan, add garlic, then onion and fry until
golden brown.
Add beaten eggs, salt and pepper to taste, sesame oil,
soy sauce and ham. Fry for 3 minutes, stirring.
Add cooked rice and continue stirring until well
mixed.
Add fried cashew nuts, stir and serve.
Serves 4.

Chicken Biriani

1kg chicken
300mL yoghurt
2 large onions
1 teaspoon ginger powder
4 cardamoms
1 teaspoon black cumin seeds
few sprigs of mint
750g rice

125g ghee
2 cloves garlic
4 cloves
1 stick cinnamon
pinch saffron strands
4 green chillies
salt to taste
water

Wash the rice and soak in cold water for 30 minutes.
Slice the onions finely.
Cut the chicken into pieces.
Soak the saffron in about 3 tablespoons milk and
water.
Put the yoghurt in a bowl, add to it the chicken and
salt and leave for 15 minutes.
Take a large pan which will fit into the oven and heat
the ghee in it; fry the sliced onions till golden brown.
Add the chicken and yoghurt and the dry spices and
cook for 15 minutes, stirring often.
Add the whole green chillies and mint sprigs.
Drain the rice and put on top of the chicken.
Grind the garlic and mix with 60mL water.
Pour this garlic water on the rice.
Pour the saffron water and the strands on top also.
Cover and bring to the boil, then put in a pre-heated
oven 150°C (300°F) for 45 minutes or more till the
rice is cooked.
Serves 8-10.
Chicken Biriani is good with vegetable curry and
Fresh Mint Chutney with Yoghurt.

Lamb Biriani

Lamb
1kg lamb chops
1½ tablespoons coriander or curry powder
1 teaspoon paprika
¼ teaspoon cumin
¼ teaspoon aniseed
¼ teaspoon each turmeric, cinnamon, cardamom
    powder, clove powder
15mm slice ginger, pounded
2 cloves garlic, crushed
1 tablespoon vinegar
1 teaspoon lemon juice
¼ teaspoon white pepper
salt
3 tablespoons cooking oil
4 large onions, chopped finely
10 almonds, pounded into a paste
6 tablespoons natural yoghurt

Rice
4 cups good long grain rice, washed and drained
3 tablespoons ghee or butter or cooking oil
2 onions, sliced finely

Chicken Biriani

thin slice ginger, shredded
1 clove garlic, shredded
6 cups water
¼ teaspoon each turmeric, cinnamon, cardamom
  powder, clove powder
1 bay leaf
salt
4 tablespoons evaporated milk
Garnish: 1 large onion, sliced and fried golden
  brown
125 g cashew nuts, fried lightly

Wash lamb, drain well, remove excess fat, place in a
bowl.
In another bowl mix coriander, paprika, cumin,
aniseed, turmeric, cinnamon, cardamom powder,
clove powder, ginger, garlic, vinegar, lemon juice,
pepper and salt to taste.
Add spice mixture to lamb and mix well. Allow to
stand for 15 minutes.
Heat 3 tablespoons cooking oil in a pan. Fry onions
till golden brown and pour into a saucepan. Add
marinated meat.
Cover saucepan and simmer with no added water for
40 minutes.
Remove from heat, add almond paste and yoghurt.

Stir to prevent sticking. Cook, covered, until liquid
has dried up and oil rises.
Remove saucepan from heat and put aside.
In a large saucepan, melt 3 tablespoons ghee and fry
onions until golden brown.
Add ginger and garlic and fry for 2 minutes.
Add rice, water, turmeric, cinnamon, cardamom
powder, clove powder, bay leaf and salt to taste. Mix
well. Bring to the boil.
Boil, covered, until rice is three-quarters cooked, then
reduce heat to low, add evaporated milk, and
continue to cook until remaining liquid is absorbed.
Remove cover, stir rice with a fork, then remove
from heat.
Transfer half the rice to a serving dish or casserole.
Spread half the curried lamb over it. Make another
layer of rice, and top dish with remaining lamb.
Cover and keep warm until serving time.
Garnish with fried onion rings and cashew nuts.
Serve with chutney and salad.
Note: This dish may be made ahead of time and
stored in the refrigerator in its casserole dish. To
reheat, sprinkle a little water over and place,
uncovered, in a medium oven 180°C (350°F) until
warmed through.
Serves 6-8.

MEAT

The most elaborate forms of cooking meat are to be found in the north of India. The simple grilled *kebab* (grilled, skewered meat) has developed so many different variations that in some places it has become customary for cooks, called *kebab chis*, to specialise in that one particular dish.

Lamb, beef and pork are all widely used in curries. Always choose good quality, lean portions. Although more expensive in this form it can be made to go a long way with the addition of vegetables, notably tomatoes and potatoes.

As a rule, 150–200g per head (for boneless cuts) should suffice — including mince, kebabs, roasts, grills and curries. A pressure cooker may be used for tougher cuts, or they can simply be cooked longer. *Kari*, or curry, is a Tamil (southern Indian) word that literally means gravy or sauce. A curry is *not* a dish — it is a class of dishes, infinitely variable according to the combination of spices used. It is not necessarily hot or very spicy.

Curried foods keep well. In fact a great number taste a lot better a day or two later. This is because the meat and spices have had time to infuse and mature. Cooking your curry a day or two earlier will prove a tasty bonus. Keep your curry dishes in the coldest part of the refrigerator — the lower shelves. Do not reheat quickly or the meat will become soft and mushy.

Basic Meat Curry (Beef, Lamb, Pork or Chicken)

1 kg lean meat or chicken
500g onions
4 cloves garlic
1 teaspoon turmeric
1 teaspoon cumin
2 teaspoons coriander
1 teaspoon ginger
2 teaspoons chilli
1 teaspoon paprika
2 teaspoons poppy seeds (optional)
120g ghee
salt to taste
2 bay leaves
150mL yoghurt or 3 tomatoes
1 teaspoon garam masala

Wash, dry and cut meat into 1-inch cubes or joint the chicken.

Minced Lamb Cutlets (p. 27)

Slice 250g onions and grind the garlic to a paste. Add to the paste 1 dessertspoon water and mix in the turmeric, cumin, coriander, ginger, chilli and paprika powders.
If poppy seeds are used, they should be ground and added to the paste.
Heat the ghee and fry the 250g sliced onions golden brown.
Lower heat, add the paste and fry for 3 or 4 minutes, stirring all the time.
Add the meat and salt and increase the heat.
Fry for 5 minutes.
Add the bay leaves and yoghurt or tomatoes (quartered), mix thoroughly, cover and simmer till the meat is almost tender.
Add garam masala and fry for 2 or 3 minutes.
Cover and simmer till ready.
If the liquid dries up while cooking, add hot water, 2 tablespoons at a time.
Stir often so that the curry does not stick to the pan.
Serve with rice or bread.
Serves 4-6.

Malai (Cream of Coconut) Curry

500g chuck steak
90g desiccated coconut
2 tablespoons coriander seeds
1 large onion
5 cloves garlic
4 tablespoons hot milk
4 large potatoes
60g ghee
1 teaspoon turmeric
¼ teaspoon chilli
½ teaspoon ginger
½ teaspoon cumin
2 teaspoons salt

Cut the meat into cubes.
Soak 60g coconut in 300mL of hot water for 10 minutes.
Squeeze and strain out the milk.
In a dry frying pan roast the coriander seeds lightly then grind them.
Slice the onion finely.
Grind the garlic to a paste.
Soak 30g coconut in hot milk.
Peel and quarter the potatoes.
Heat the ghee and brown the onion and add all the spices and cook for 3 minutes.
Then add the coconut and milk mixture, meat and salt and simmer for 5 minutes.
Add the coconut milk and bring to the boil.

Add the potatoes and simmer till both meat and potatoes are ready.
Add lemon.
If more gravy is required, add a little water to thin down liquid.
Serve this mild curry with boiled rice.
Serves 4-6.

Pork Curry

4 tablespoons cooking oil
½ teaspoon mustard seed
1 large onion, minced
thin slice ginger, pounded
1 clove garlic, chopped finely
4 potatoes, quartered
2 tablespoons coriander or curry powder
½ teaspoon chilli paste (optional)
½ teaspoon pepper
salt
1 cup water
¼ teaspoon each clove powder, cardamom
   powder, cinnamon, turmeric, cumin
1 tablespoon tomato paste
750g lean pork, cut into 25mm cubes
1 teaspoon vinegar

Heat oil in a saucepan, add mustard seed, fry for 2 seconds only, then add onion and fry until golden brown.
Add ginger, garlic, potatoes, coriander, chilli paste (optional), pepper, salt to taste, water, clove powder, cardamom powder, cinnamon, turmeric and cumin. Mix well.
Cover, bring to the boil and boil until potatoes are half cooked, then add tomato paste, pork and vinegar. Mix well.
Reduce heat to low and simmer, covered for 1 hour or until potatoes and pork are cooked.
Remove lid and bring to the boil, then remove pan from heat.
Serve with rice and vegetables.
Mild.
Serves 4-6.

Korma Curry

500g lean lamb or beef
150mL yoghurt
1½ tablespoons poppy seeds
lemon juice to taste
a few sprigs green coriander leaves (if available)
2 cloves garlic
2 large onions
⅛ fresh coconut

4 green chillies
3 teaspoons coriander powder
¼ teaspoon ginger powder
¼ teaspoon cinnamon powder
¼ teaspoon clove powder
¼ teaspoon cumin
120g ghee
1 teaspoon chilli powder
salt to taste

Wash and cut the meat into 2.5cm pieces.
Put the yoghurt in a bowl and whisk till smooth.
Slice the onions finely.
Grate the coconut.
Grind the coconut, garlic, poppy seeds and ginger to a paste and mix in all the powdered spices.
Heat the ghee and fry the onions until they are a crisp, golden brown.
Drain the onions, crush them and add them to the yoghurt.
Add the paste to the ghee and fry over low heat for 5 minutes.
Add meat, yoghurt mixture and salt; bring to the boil then simmer over low heat for 1 hour or till the meat is tender and the curry is a rich brown.
Sprinkle over the cumin and fry for 5 minutes.
Add the green chillies whole or sliced and the coriander leaves; cover and remove from the heat.
Before serving add the lemon juice and more salt if required.
Medium.
Serves 4.
Goes well with Pilau Rice.

Hot Beef Chilli Curry

500g lean meat
1 lump of tamarind pulp the size of a walnut
2 medium onions
2 cloves garlic
2 or 3 green chillies
60g ghee
1 teaspoon cumin
1 teaspoon turmeric
2 teaspoons chilli
1 teaspoon ginger
salt to taste

Soak the tamarind in 2 tablespoons water.
Cut the meat into 2.5cm cubes.
Slice the onions finely and chop the garlic.
Chop the green chillies.
Heat the ghee and fry the onions and garlic till lightly browned.
Lower heat and add the spices and green chillies and cook, covered, for 5 minutes.
Add the meat and salt and stir thoroughly, then cover

and cook for 10 minutes.

Add 150mL warm water and simmer 1 hour or till the meat is tender.

Squeeze the tamarind and strain the juice.

Add this juice to the curry and fry for 5 to 6 minutes till the gravy is thick.

This is a very hot curry and is served with plain boiled rice.

Serves 4.

Keema (or Mince) Curry

4 tablespoons cooking oil
2 large onions, chopped finely
1 clove garlic, chopped finely
thin slice ginger, shredded
2 potatoes, cut into 15 mm cubes
¼ cup water
750 g minced beef or lamb or pork
¼ teaspoon each cinnamon, clove powder, cardamom powder, turmeric
salt and pepper
2 tablespoons coriander or curry powder
½ teaspoon chilli powder
½ teaspoon aniseed
½ teaspoon cumin
½ cup frozen peas
125 g coconut cream or 4 tablespoons evaporated milk

Heat oil in a large saucepan, fry onions until golden brown.

Add garlic and ginger and fry for 2 minutes.

Add potatoes, stir, add water and cook gently, covered, for about 10 minutes, stirring occasionally.

Add minced meat, cinnamon, clove powder, cardamom powder, turmeric, salt and pepper to taste, coriander, chilli powder, aniseed and cumin. Mix well and stir constantly to prevent burning.

Continue frying and stirring until water is absorbed, then add frozen peas and coconut cream or evaporated milk. Mix well.

Cook until peas are cooked and curry is dry, stirring constantly.

Remove to a dish and serve hot with rice and vegetables or bread.

Note: 1 tomato, chopped, or 1 teaspoon tomato paste may be added with the peas and coconut cream, if desired.

Serves 4-6.

Korma Lamb Curry

Meat and Coconut Curry

1 kg leg of lamb or topside or round steak cut into
   25 mm cubes or as desired
2 tablespoons coriander or curry powder
½ teaspoon chilli powder (optional)
¼ teaspoon black pepper
¼ teaspoon each turmeric, cumin, aniseed,
   cinnamon, clove powder, cardamom powder
1 clove garlic, pounded
5 mm slice ginger, shredded
1 teaspoon vinegar
2 fresh green chillies, slit open (optional)
salt
3 or 4 curry leaves
½ cup water
2 tablespoons cooking oil
1 large onion, sliced finely
2 ripe tomatoes, quartered
125 g coconut cream mixed with 1½ cups water

Put meat in a saucepan, add coriander, chilli powder
(optional), black pepper, turmeric, cumin, aniseed,
cinnamon, clove powder, cardamom powder, garlic,
ginger, vinegar, green chillies (optional), salt to taste,
curry leaves and water. Mix well.
Bring to the boil, reduce heat and boil slowly,
covered, until meat is cooked.
In a frying pan, heat oil, add sliced onion, and fry
until golden brown.
Add tomatoes, toss and turn for 5 seconds, then pour
contents of pan into the boiled meat. Stir well, add
coconut cream and water, and mix again. Bring to the
boil and remove from heat.
Serve hot with rice, bread and salad.
Note: Boiled potatoes may be added to the curry
before serving, if desired.
Serves 4-6.

Lamb Curry with Cabbage

1 medium sized cabbage
500 g lean lamb
2 teaspoons coriander
1 teaspoon turmeric
1 teaspoon ginger
2 cloves garlic (mashed)

Hot Beef Chilli Curry (p. 24)

¼ teaspoon chilli
250 g tomatoes
2 teaspoons salt
2 onions
60 g ghee
juice of 1 lemon
150 mL yoghurt

Cut the cabbage in thin slices and steep in cold, salted
water for 30 minutes.
Cube the meat and place in saucepan.
Add spices, yoghurt, chopped tomatoes, salt and
300 mL water and mix well together.
Slice the onions thinly and place on top.
Over these place the slices of cabbage, well drained,
and then the ghee.
Bring to the boil, and then simmer gently until the
ingredients are well cooked and the liquid is
absorbed.
Squeeze in the lemon juice and simmer for a further
10 minutes.
Mild.
Serves 4.

Minced Lamb Cutlets

1 large potato
4 cloves garlic
1 large onion
1 green capsicum
1 tablespoon chopped parsley
500 g lamb, minced
¼ teaspoon turmeric
½ teaspoon ginger
1 teaspoon cumin
4 eggs
salt and pepper to taste
breadcrumbs
2 tablespoons oil

Boil and mash potato.
Crush garlic cloves.
Chop onion, capsicum and parsley.
Combine these ingredients with the mince, spices and
1 egg in a bowl.
Mix thoroughly, preferably with your hand.
Season to taste and leave for at least 1 hour.
Beat together remaining 3 eggs.
Take a portion of mixture and shape into a cutlet.
Dip in beaten egg and coat with breadcrumbs.
Heat oil and fry the cutlets on medium heat for about
5 minutes each side or till meat is cooked and brown
on both sides.
Remove and keep hot in oven till all the cutlets are
cooked.
Serve with tomato sauce, salad and vegetables.
Serves 4.

Spicy and Sour Meat

500g lean beef
3 cloves garlic
2 medium onions
½ teaspoon garam masala
¼ teaspoon ginger
½ teaspoon turmeric
2 teaspoons cumin
3 tablespoons vinegar
30g ghee

Cut meat into cubes.
Crush garlic cloves and mix with sliced onion, spices and 2 tablespoons vinegar.
Heat the ghee and fry the spice mixture for 5 minutes, stirring constantly.
Put in the meat cubes and fry until brown, stirring constantly to prevent burning. Serve with Pilav or Saffron Rice.
Add the rest of the vinegar to the water and add to the fried meat and spices.
Cover and simmer on a very low heat for about 1 hour or till meat is tender.
Stir occasionally to prevent sticking and burning.
Serve with Pilau or Saffron Rice.
Mild.
Serves 4.

Kashmiri Kofta Curry

3 green chillies
750g lean mince
3 tablespoons yoghurt
1 teaspoon ginger
½ teaspoon coriander
1 teaspoon chilli powder
2 teaspoons garam masala
120g ghee
1 teaspoon sugar
1 tablespoon dried milk
salt to taste
1 teaspoon pepper
2 green cardamoms
300mL warm water

Chop the green chillies very finely.
Put the mince in a bowl and add the chopped chillies, 1 tablespoon yoghurt, ginger, coriander, chilli powder, 1 teaspoon garam masala, 30g ghee and salt to taste.
Mix thoroughly and shape into small sausages.
Heat the rest of the ghee in a saucepan; add the sugar, dried milk, 2 tablespoons yoghurt, 1 teaspoon garam masala and salt to taste.

Fry and add 150mL warm water and the meat koftas. Simmer till the water has evaporated then turn the koftas and add another 150mL of warm water. Simmer till water is absorbed.
Sprinkle with pepper and the coarsely ground cardamom. Serve with Saffron rice.
Medium.
Serves 4-6.

Kofta Curry

For Koftas:
1 dessertspoon mint leaves
1 medium onion
2 cloves garlic
500g fine mince
2 teaspoons salt
¼ teaspoon ginger powder
¼ teaspoon chilli
¼ teaspoon clove powder

For Curry:
1 inch piece fresh ginger
1 tomato
2 cloves garlic
½ teaspoon ginger powder
1 medium onion
60g ghee
600mL yoghurt
1 dessertspoon coriander
150mL water

Chop the mint finely. Chop one onion and 2 cloves garlic. Put the mince in a bowl with the mint, chopped garlic and onion. Mix and add the salt, chilli, clove and ginger powders (¼ teaspoon each).
Make into balls the size of a large walnut. Peel the ginger and chop very finely. Chop the tomato coarsely, crush the garlic and add to 150mL of water and rest of ginger powder. Slice the onion finely.
Heat the ghee and fry onion till cream coloured. Add the tomato, yoghurt and coriander powder and simmer for 15 minutes. Add the garlic water and simmer for 5 minutes and add the meat balls.
Cover and cook gently for 45 minutes or till the meat is cooked. If more gravy is required add 150mL hot water and simmer for 5 minutes more. Serve with boiled rice or Coconut Rice and bread.
Mild.
Serves 4.

Spicy and Sour Meat

Pork Vindaloo

Pork Vindaloo

This dish is a southern Indian delicacy, usually very hot and sour.

1 kg pork
3 large onions
5 cloves garlic
2 large cardamoms
8 cloves
20 peppercorns
3 tablespoons vinegar
3 teaspoons chilli powder
1 teaspoon cinnamon powder
2 teaspoons cumin powder
2 teaspoons turmeric powder
2 teaspoons mustard powder
1 teaspoon ginger powder
salt to taste
4 tablespoons mustard oil

Grind 2 onions, garlic, cardamom seeds, cloves and peppercorns to a paste with a little vinegar.

Kashmiri Kofta Curry (p. 28)

Mix into this paste all the powdered spices; add vinegar to keep moist.
Wash, dry and cut the pork into 3 cm pieces. Put the meat into a bowl and marinate with a quarter of the paste and salt to taste.
Pour all the vinegar over the meat and leave for 5 to 6 hours.
Slice the remaining onion finely.
Heat the oil till it smokes, then cool.
Put on a medium heat and fry the onions and ginger till light brown, add the masala paste and fry till the raw smell disappears.
Add the pork mixture and simmer over a low heat for about 1 hour or till the meat is tender.
This curry can be kept for a few days.
No water should be used when cooking the vindaloo.
This is a hot curry. For a milder effect use less chilli powder (1 teaspoon for mild, 2 teaspoons for medium).
Serve with boiled rice and Cucumber and Pineapple or Tomato Salad.
Serves 6-8.

Kebabs

Kebabs can be made from minced or cubed meat and are either barbecued or fried. Essentially dry they are best served with salads and parathas.

1 teaspoon powdered poppy seed
1 teaspoon ginger
2 teaspoons coriander
1 teaspoon turmeric
¼ teaspoon chilli
1 teaspoon salt
1 teaspoon onion juice
2 teaspoons yoghurt
500g lamb, beef or pork cut in cubes
30g ghee

Mix all the spices including the onion juice. (Onion juice is extracted by chopping an onion, putting it in a mortar with 2 teaspoons cold water and pounding carefully. Then squeeze the whole through a piece of muslin or a very fine sieve.)
Add the yoghurt.
Soak the meat in boiling water for 5 minutes, then remove and drain it.
Mix the meat well with the yoghurt and spices.
Make sure that all the cubes are well coated.
Let stand for 30 minutes.
Thread on metal skewers.
Grill under a preheated grill and baste continuously with the melted fat till done. Grill gently so that meat is tender and cooked through.
Collect the gravy which forms at the bottom of the pan to serve with the grilled meat on a bed of Saffron Rice.
Serves 4-6.

Beef Malaysian Style

750g topside steak cut into 25mm cubes
¼ teaspoon white pepper
¼ teaspoon cinnamon
¼ teaspoon clove powder
salt
1 teaspoon sugar
3 tablespoons cooking oil
1 large onion, cut into 15mm slices
thin slice ginger, shredded
1 tablespoon chilli sauce (optional)
¼ cup water
2 tablespoons soy sauce
leaves of 3 shallots, chopped
½ cucumber, peeled and diced (optional)

Put beef in a bowl. Add white pepper, cinnamon, clove powder, salt to taste and sugar and mix well.
Heat oil in a large pan, add onion and fry until lightly browned.
Add ginger, seasoned beef, chilli sauce (optional) and

Seekh Kebabs

water and mix well. Bring to the boil, reduce heat and simmer, covered, for 1 hour or until meat is tender. Remove lid, add soy sauce and fry until gravy is thick.
Add shallot leaves and cucumber (optional), mix well and serve with rice and salad.
Serves 4-6.

Seekh Kebabs

1 lemon
1 onion
1 tomato
1 egg
500g very finely minced meat
1 teaspoon coriander
½ teaspoon cumin
¼ teaspoon chilli
½ teaspoon garam masala
1 teaspoon salt
45g ghee

Slice lemon in rounds, removing pips.
Slice onion in rings and separate them.
Scald, skin and slice tomato.
Set these aside.
Mix the egg and mince well in a bowl.
Add the spices and salt.
Apply some grease to fingers and skewers, and fold meat in a long cigar shape on the skewers evenly.
Brush well with cooking fat and grill gently under low grill in greased grilling pan.
Turn skewers often so that the meat is browned evenly all over.
When kebabs are ready slide them gently off skewers so that they do not break.
Serve at once in a hot dish as a starter or a main course with the lemon slices, onion rings and tomato slices arranged around them.
Serves 4-6.

Liver Kebabs

1kg lamb's fry
juice of 2 lemons
2 teaspoons chilli powder
salt to taste
butter or oil for basting

Wash and dry liver and cut into 2cm pieces.
Marinate the pieces in lemon juice, chilli powder and salt for 1 hour.
Thread the liver pieces onto skewers and grill gently, basting with butter or oil.
Serve with Saffron Rice and Fresh Tomato Chutney.
Serves 6-8.

POULTRY

Some of the most famous Indian dishes are based on chicken. Murgh Mussallam, for instance — whole, roasted and elaborately spiced chicken cooked in yoghurt — is an old and favourite feast and banquet dish. Mulligatawny, a chicken soup, and Country Captain, a curry, formed the backbone of the British diet in Indian colonial days. They continue to be popular.

Although mostly chicken recipes have been given, the same recipes can be used for cooking game birds. Pheasants, partridges and quails are extremely popular.

Poultry may be baked — whole or in pieces — barbecued, fried, stewed or steamed. For many of the dishes requiring the chicken to be jointed, you may like to save time by buying chicken pieces rather than a whole bird.

Frozen chickens are convenient, readily available and less expensive than fresh — but they are, in general, inferior in flavour. A fresh chicken will give a much better result — particularly in the baked and fried dishes — so it is worth spending the little extra time and money to obtain one.

Madras Chicken Curry

1 chicken, jointed
60g ghee
2 tablespoons chopped onions
2 cloves garlic, chopped
1½ tablespoons curry powder
a little water or stock
salt and lemon juice to taste
250g fresh tomatoes (optional)

Fry lightly in 60g of ghee, 2 tablespoons chopped onions, and 2 cloves of garlic chopped.
Cook until the onions begin to change colour, then add 1½ tablespoons curry powder.
Stir well and fry for 3-4 minutes.
Now add the jointed chicken, stir thoroughly. Cover the pan and cook slowly for as long as possible without adding any moisture.
Should the curry get too dry, add gradually a little water or stock to make thick gravy.
Simmer slowly until the meat is tender, and the oil comes to the surface.
Add salt and lemon juice to taste and serve with Pilau Rice.
As a variation you can add a tablespoonful of tomato paste or 250g fresh tomatoes, chopped, whilst the meat is cooking.
Medium.
Serves 4-6.

Chicken Curry with Sliced Coconut (p. 36)

Sri Lankan Chicken Curry

1 chicken, jointed
1 onion and 2 cloves of garlic (finely minced)
3-4 fresh green or red or pickled chillies, cut lengthwise
1 teaspoon ground turmeric
1 dessertspoon ground coriander seeds or a handful fresh coriander leaves
600mL of thin coconut milk
2 tablespoons of thick coconut milk
1 tablespoon ghee
a little lemon juice

Warm the ghee and add all the ingredients except the chicken and coconut milk.
Fry for 2-3 minutes.
Add the chicken and 600mL of thin coconut milk.
Simmer slowly for about 45 minutes or until the chicken is tender, then add the thick coconut milk.
Salt to taste and add a squeeze of lemon juice.
Simmer for another 5 minutes with the pan uncovered.
Mild.
Serves 4-6.

Chicken Malai Curry

1 onion
2 cloves of garlic
1 tablespoon ghee
1 jointed chicken
600mL of thin coconut milk
1 tablespoon of thick coconut milk
salt to taste
a little lemon juice

For the curry mixture:
1 tablespoon ground coriander
1 teaspoon ground mustard seed
1 teaspoon ground cumin seed
1 teaspoon ground turmeric
½ teaspoon ground ginger
½ teaspoon ground chillies
Mix above ingredients together.

Cook but do not brown, 1 onion and 2 cloves of garlic, finely chopped, in 1 tablespoon of ghee.
Add the curry mixture and the jointed chicken and fry for 5 minutes
To make the gravy add enough thin coconut milk to cover the chicken.
Simmer gently with the pan uncovered for about 45 minutes or until the gravy begins to thicken and the chicken is tender.
Add a tablespoon of thick coconut milk.

Dry Chicken Curry

Salt to taste and add a squeeze of lemon juice and serve with Saffron or boiled rice.
Mild.
Serves 4-6.

Chicken Curry with Sliced Coconut

1 chicken, jointed
½ a fresh coconut, sliced and with the outer skin removed
1 onion, minced finely
2 garlic cloves, minced finely
2 cardamoms
2 cloves
1 5 cm stick of cinnamon
1 heaped tablespoon of curry powder
1 dessertspoon of curry paste
60 g ghee
250 g fresh tomatoes, peeled and chopped
300 mL water
salt to taste
squeeze of lemon juice

Fry lightly for 2 or 3 minutes in ghee the onions, garlic and spices.
Add the curry powder and curry paste.

Mix thoroughly and continue to fry for another 3-4 minutes.
Add the tomato and jointed chicken, sliced coconut and 300 mL of water to form a thick gravy.
Mix thoroughly, cover the pan tightly, and simmer until the chicken is tender.
Add salt and a squeeze of lemon juice to taste and serve with Tomato Rice.
Mild.
Serves 4-6.

Dry Chicken Curry

1 chicken, jointed
2 onions finely sliced
2 cloves of garlic finely sliced
2 dessertspoons of curry paste
1 dessertspoon of tomato paste
60 g ghee
salt to taste
squeeze of lemon juice
1 tablespoon desiccated coconut

Fry lightly in the ghee for 2-3 minutes the onions and garlic. Add the curry and tomato paste, and continue to fry for another 2-3 minutes.
Add the chicken.
Mix well, cover the pan tightly and simmer for about 45 minutes or until the chicken is cooked.
Note: The pan must be continually watched, as the

contents are likely to stick. If this appears likely, add just sufficient water to prevent it.

Add salt and lemon juice to taste, and 1 tablespoon of finely desiccated coconut which will absorb any excess gravy.

Serve with chapatis and salad.

Mild.

Serves 4-6.

Madras Duck Curry (Vathoo)

1 duck, jointed
60g ghee
1 onion finely sliced
1 clove garlic finely sliced
2 or 3 fresh chillies
3 dessertspoons curry powder
½ teaspoon cumin seed
sufficient water for gravy
salt to taste
squeeze lemon juice
1 tablespoon thick coconut milk
water

Fry onion and garlic, both finely sliced, and 2 or 3 fresh chillies cut in half lengthwise in the ghee.

Add 3 dessertspoons of curry powder (or curry paste)

and ½ teaspoon of cumin seed.

Mix thoroughly and continue the cooking for 3 or 4 minutes. Now add the jointed duck.

Stir the whole thoroughly and add sufficient water to form a thick gravy.

Cover the pan closely and simmer for about 1 hour or until the duck is cooked.

Add salt and lemon juice to taste and 1 tablespoon of thick coconut milk just before serving.

Mild.

Serves 4-6.

Spiced Chicken and Yoghurt

1 × 1.5 kg chicken
1 large onion
3 cloves garlic
1 teaspoon ginger powder
60g ghee
1 teaspoon salt
450mL yoghurt
1 bunch coriander or watercress
¼ green capsicum
½ teaspoon turmeric
1 teaspoon garam masala
900mL hot water

Spiced Chicken and Yoghurt

Wash and joint the chicken.
Slice the onion finely.
Grind the garlic to a paste and mix with the ginger powder.
Heat the ghee and brown the onion.
Add the garlic, ginger paste and salt and cook for 5 minutes.
Now add the chicken pieces and brown well.
Add 900 mL hot water and simmer for about 45 minutes or till the chicken is tender and about 4 tablespoons gravy remain.
Add the yoghurt and the coriander or watercress leaves, the sliced green capsicum, turmeric and garam masala and stir thoroughly.
Bring to the boil and remove at once.
Mild.
Serves 4-6.

Southern Curried Chicken

1 × 1 kg chicken
10 dry red chillies
2 tablespoons poppy seeds
2 tablespoons coriander seeds
½ teaspoon cumin seeds
6 cashew nuts
1 teaspoon turmeric
1 fresh coconut
90g ghee
4 small onions
4 cloves garlic
½ teaspoon ginger powder
salt to taste
juice of 1 lemon
750mL hot water

Grind the chillies, poppy seeds, coriander, cumin and cashew nuts to a paste and mix in the turmeric.
Cut the chicken into pieces.
Grate the coconut.
Put in a bowl and pour over 150 mL hot water.
Squeeze out the coconut milk and reserve.
Pour 600mL hot water over the coconut and let it soak.
Heat the ghee and fry the onions, garlic, ginger, ground spices, chicken and salt till they are brown.
Squeeze the juice from the coconut and pour over the chicken.
Simmer over low heat till the chicken is tender.
Just before serving, add the thick coconut milk and the lemon juice.
If fresh ginger is used it should be ground with the other spices.
Serve with Saffron Rice.
Hot.
Serves 4-6.

Country Captain (Bhoona Moorgee)

1 boiled fowl (do not over-cook)
2 small chopped onions
60g ghee
2 green chillies
6 thin slices green ginger
1 clove garlic, sliced
½ teaspoon turmeric
salt to taste
chicken stock

Joint the chicken or remove flesh from bones.
Fry onions and garlic in the ghee over a medium heat.
Add ginger, chillies, turmeric and chicken.
Fry till the chicken browns slightly.
Add a little stock.
Season with salt to taste.
Simmer until flavours are well blended.
Note: Crisp fried onions are an excellent garnish for this dish.
Mild.
Serves 4-6.

Chicken Curry with Cashews

1 x 1.5kg chicken
3 tablespoons ghee
2 onions finely chopped
3 cloves garlic finely chopped
1½ teaspoons finely grated ginger
3 tablespoons curry powder
1 teaspoon chilli powder
3 teaspoons salt
3 ripe tomatoes, peeled
2 tablespoons chopped fresh coriander or mint
2 teaspoons garam masala
125mL natural yoghurt
190mL raw cashews finely ground

Cut chicken into serving pieces.
Heat ghee in a large saucepan and gently fry onion, garlic and ginger until soft and golden, stirring occasionally.
Add curry powder, chilli powder and salt and stir.
Add tomatoes.
Add chopped herbs and chicken, stirring well to coat chicken with the curry mixture.
Cover tightly and simmer 45 minutes or until chicken is tender.

Chicken Curry with Cashews

Stir in garam masala and yoghurt, simmer 5 minutes, gently, or yoghurt will curdle.
Stir in cashews and heat through.
Serve with rice, salad and parathas.
Mild.
Serves 4-6.

Bombay Chicken Curry

1 x 2 kg chicken, jointed
2 tablespoons vinegar
125 g desiccated coconut
4 cloves garlic
½ teaspoon cumin powder
½ teaspoon turmeric
1 teaspoon chilli powder
½ teaspoon ground pepper
2 tablespoons olive oil
1 teaspoon ginger
10 curry leaves
2 teaspoons salt
1½ dessertspoons sugar

Boil the chicken and reserve liquid. Mix or grind together the vinegar, coconut, garlic, cumin, turmeric, chilli and pepper.
Heat the oil in a saucepan and gently fry the mixed spices.
Add the ginger and curry leaves and fry for 2 minutes.
Add the chicken pieces and 300 mL stock (reserved liquid).
Simmer for 15 minutes, then add the salt and sugar and remove from the fire after stirring.
This can be eaten hot or cold.
Mild.
Serves 4-6.

Spiced Grilled Chicken

1 x 2 kg chicken
½ teaspoon garlic
½ teaspoon ginger
½ teaspoon chilli
¼ teaspoon curry powder
1 pinch pepper
¼ teaspoon turmeric
1 teaspoon salt
30 g ghee

Apricot Chicken

Clean, wash and joint the chicken and prick all over with a fork.
Mix all the other ingredients except the ghee, rub well into the chicken pieces and marinate for 2 hours.
Then brush all over with melted ghee, cook briefly under griller to seal the juices in and then gently simmer for 45 minutes or until chicken is cooked and tender.
Serve hot with lemon slices and salad.
Mild.
Serves 4-6.

Apricot Chicken

1 x 1.5 kg chicken
250 g apricots
2 medium onions
2 medium tomatoes
2 cloves garlic
½ teaspoon ginger
¼ teaspoon chilli
¼ teaspoon saffron
1 tablespoon hot milk
2 tablespoons ghee
¼ teaspoon garam masala
2 teaspoons salt
900 mL warm water

Wash, clean and joint the chicken.
Stone the apricots.
Chop the onions finely.
Blanch, skin and chop the tomatoes coarsely.
Pound garlic into a paste with the ginger and chilli.
Crumple the saffron into the hot milk and let it dissolve.
In a saucepan heat the fat and fry the onions till a light cream colour.
Put in the garlic, ginger, and chilli paste and fry with the onions 5 minutes, stirring often.
Now add the chicken pieces, garam masala, tomatoes and salt to the pan.
Pour in 900 mL warm water and simmer gently for about 45 minutes or until chicken is cooked and tender.
Remove cover now and again to see that water has not evaporated. If it has add a little warm water.
When chicken is tender, add the saffron milk and apricots and cook gently until apricots are soft and tender. Serve hot.
Note: Duck or any other poultry can be cooked like this with peaches or apricots. Tinned fruit can be used, but not the syrup.
Serve with salad and boiled rice.
Mild.
Serves 4-6.

Chicken Vindaloo

1 x 1.5 kg chicken
1 teaspoon mustard seed
6 cloves garlic
2 large onions
2 teaspoons turmeric
1 teaspoon ginger
1 cinnamon stick
2 teaspoons chilli
2 teaspoons cumin
6 cloves
2½ tablespoons vinegar
1 tablespoon brown sugar
salt to taste
90g ghee

Wash and dry the chicken and cut into pieces.
Grind the mustard seeds
Grind the garlic and 1 onion to a paste.
Slice the other onion.
Put the chicken in a bowl with all the spices and the vinegar, sugar and salt and marinate for 4 hours.
Heat the ghee and fry the onion. Add the chicken and the paste and simmer for 45 minutes or till the chicken is tender.
The saucepan must be covered with a tight fitting lid while simmering.
Serve with boiled or Pilau rice.
Medium.
Serves 4-6.

Mulligatawny Soup

Though called a soup, Mulligatawny is a meal in itself and can be served as a main course.

10 peppercorns
½ teaspoon ginger
2 teaspoons turmeric
1 tablespoon coriander
1 teaspoon chilli
1 onion
1 small boiling chicken
2 tablespoons ghee
salt to taste
1 lemon
1200mL water

Grind the peppercorns and mix with the powdered spices.
Moisten them with a little water to make a paste.
Slice the onion finely.
Joint the chicken and simmer in the water for 10 minutes. Add the paste and simmer till the chicken pieces are tender.
Strain the soup.
Heat the ghee in a clean pan and fry the onion till golden brown.
Add to this the soup and meat.
Season with salt and bring to the boil once.
Serve with boiled rice and lemon slices.
Medium.
Serves 4-6.

Curried Duck

1 large onion
3 tablespoons coriander seeds
1 teaspoon cumin seeds
½ teaspoon fenugreek seeds
1 teaspoon poppy seeds
4 cloves garlic
1 inch piece green ginger
1½ teaspoons turmeric
½ fresh coconut
90g ghee
1 small duck
1 teaspoon chilli powder
salt to taste
1 lemon
600mL water

Slice the onion.
In a dry frying pan roast the coriander, cumin, fenugreek and poppy seeds. Do not let them burn.
Grind the garlic, ginger and the roasted spices to a paste and add the turmeric.
Grate the coconut and soak it in 300mL boiling water for 1 hour.
Squeeze and take out the milk.
Strain.
Joint the duck.
Fry the onion in the ghee and when golden brown add the paste and fry over a low heat for 3 minutes.
Add the duck and fry for another 3 minutes.
Cover and cook for 5 minutes over gentle heat then add 300mL warm water, chilli powder and salt and simmer for about 45 minutes or till duck is tender.
Ten minutes before serving add the coconut milk and the juice of the lemon.
Serve with rice.
Medium.
Serves 4.

Curried Duck

Murgh Mussallam

1 x 1.5 kg chicken
3 large onions
4 cloves garlic
1 tablespoon poppy seeds
2 black cardamoms
½ teaspoon cumin seeds
2 teaspoons cumin ⎤
¼ teaspoon clove powder ⎥
1 teaspoon ginger ⎥ masala
1 teaspoon cinnamon ⎥ paste
½ teaspoon black pepper ⎥
1 teaspoon chilli ⎦
salt to taste
125 g ghee
450 mL yoghurt

Truss the chicken, wash and clean.
Slice onions finely.
Grind the garlic, poppy seeds, cardamoms and cumin seeds to a paste.
Add all the other spices to the paste and a little water.
Rub the chicken with the paste after adding salt.
Heat the ghee in a heavy saucepan and fry the onions a golden brown.
Remove crisp onions and keep aside.
In the same fat fry the chicken with the masala paste.
Beat the yoghurt till smooth and add the fried onions.
Pour this over the chicken, bring to the boil, then simmer for about 45 minutes or till the chicken is tender.
Uncover and fry for a few minutes till the water is absorbed.
Serve with roti.
Medium.
Serves 4-6.

Chicken Cutlets

1 chicken
2-3 cloves garlic
½ green capsicum
2 teaspoons salt
2 teaspoons ginger
3 eggs
breadcrumbs
oil for deep drying

Cut the chicken into pieces and remove the bones.
Put the fillets in a muslin cloth and flatten with a meat tenderiser.

Chicken Cutlets

Grind or mash the garlic and green capsicum together.
Add the salt and ginger and apply the mixture to both sides of the cutlets.
Allow to stand for 5 to 6 hours.
When cutlets are ready to cook dip them into the lightly beaten eggs, coat with breadcrumbs and deep fry.
Mild.
Serves 4-6.

Chicken Kebabs

1 x 1.5 kg chicken
2 medium onions
3 cloves garlic
4 cloves
4 peppercorns
8 tablespoons yoghurt
½ teaspoon ginger powder
1 teaspoon chilli powder
½ tablespoon vinegar
salt to taste
butter for basting

Grind the onions, garlic, cloves and peppercorns to a paste.
Put the yoghurt in a large bowl and mix in the paste and all the other ingredients.
Prick the chicken all over with a fork and rub in the yoghurt mixture.
Leave the chicken to marinate in the bowl for 1-2 hours.
Put on a rotary spit and baste with butter.
If you do not have a spit, preheat oven to 190°C (375°F) and roast the chicken in the usual way, basting with butter from time to time.
Note: This is generally eaten with chapatis or parathas and a salad of sliced onions in lemon juice and may be served as a starter or a main course.
Mild.
Serves 4-6.

Tandoori Chicken

Tandoori chicken is traditionally cooked in a special kind of oven known as a 'Tandoor'. Charcoal is put inside an earthenware oven and made red hot. The chicken or meat is put inside on skewers. The meats cooked in these ovens are superb; no other method gives you the same delicious flavour. Good results however can be achieved in your kitchen oven or on a rotary spit.

1 x 1 kg roasting chicken
1 large onion

4 cloves garlic
½ teaspoon ginger powder
1 teaspoon coriander powder
½ teaspoon chilli powder
2 teaspoons salt
150mL yoghurt
1 tablespoon vinegar
1 tablespoon Worcestershire sauce
2 lemons
30g melted butter
1 teaspoon garam masala

Clean the chicken, keep whole but do not truss.
Make 3 or 4 cuts on each side of the bird.
Grind the onion and garlic to a paste; add the ginger, coriander, cumin, chilli and salt.
Beat the yoghurt in a bowl and add the paste, vinegar, Worcestershire sauce and the juice of 1 lemon. Mix thoroughly and rub on the chicken. Marinate the chicken for a minimum of six hours and preferably for 24 to 48 hours in the coolest part of the refrigerator. Remove all excess marinade and roast in a moderate oven for 20 minutes or till the chicken is tender. If possible cook on a barbecue rotary spit. Brush with melted butter, sprinkle over garam masala and lemon juice and serve.
Serve with salad and chapatis (Lebanese bread or Greek 'pitta' bread is an excellent alternative but should be warmed gently.)
Mild.
Serves 4-6.

Tandoori Chicken (p. 45)   *Prawn Cutlets (p. 48)*

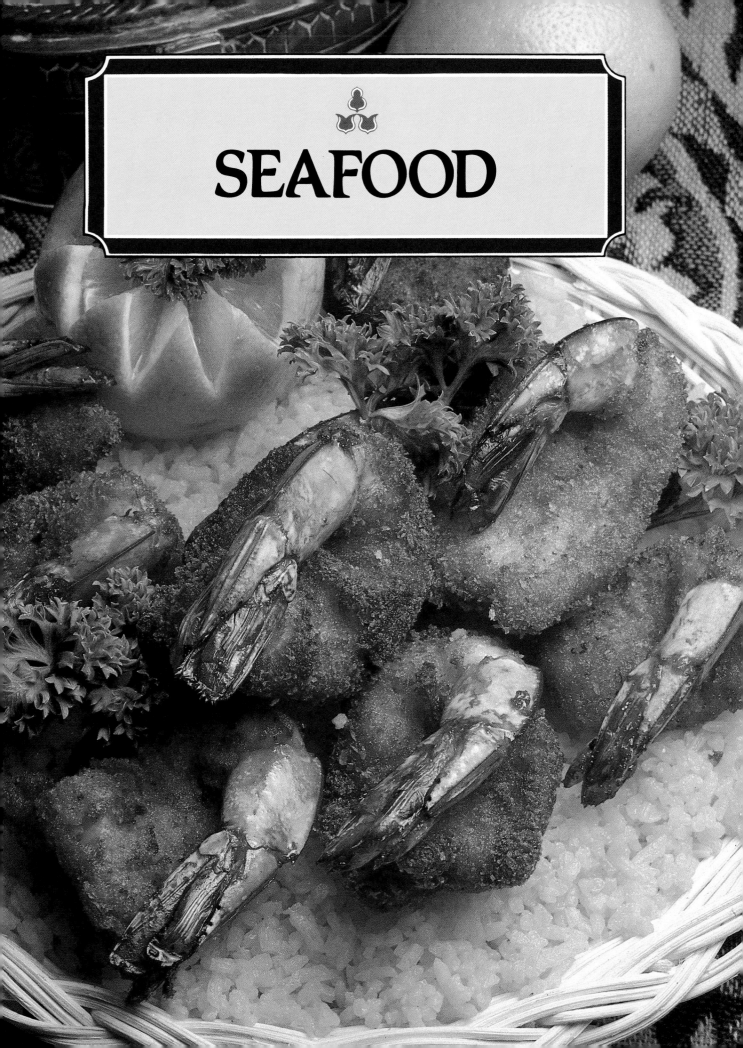

SEAFOOD

The usual method of cooking seafood in India is to curry it, and, even when fried, it is flavoured with curry spices. Most types of seafood can be used including crabs, lobster, prawns and firm fish fillets (such as jewfish, bream and snapper).

Always buy fresh fish. The gills should be bright red, the eyes clear, the skin shiny and the body firm and taut. There should be no pronounced fishy odour. Fish curries should not be frozen. The all-too-tender flesh does not reheat well, and will usually fall to pieces.

Whereas European cooks often flour and batter fish fillets, the Indian cook marinates fillets in spices, yoghurt, or lime or lemon juice. This gives a distinctive piquancy while still retaining the fresh, natural flavour of the fish.

It is important not to overcook seafood — this would spoil the delicate flavour and texture of the flesh. As soon as the fish is tender and easy to flake it should be removed from the heat.

Prawn Cutlets

8 large prawns
2 medium onions
½ teaspoon ginger
½ teaspoon chilli powder

salt to taste
1 egg
breadcrumbs
oil for frying

Remove shells from prawns but keep the tails.
Slit the prawns down the back and remove the sand track.
Wash and dry the prawns and place on a board.
Gash the prawns and flatten slightly.
Grind the onions to a paste and add the ginger, chilli and salt.
Smear this paste over the flattened prawns, then dip them in beaten egg and coat with breadcrumbs.
Fry in shallow fat for a few minutes.
Serve with salad.
Serves 4.

Baked Fish Fillets

500 g white fish cut into serving pieces
4 red chillies (seeds removed) — chopped finely
2 slices green ginger chopped finely
2 cloves garlic chopped finely
1 medium onion chopped finely
2 teaspoons lemon or lime juice
1 teaspoon turmeric
1 teaspoon sugar
salt

Baked Fish Fillets

Fish Kebabs

Salt the fish fillets lightly.
Combine all other ingredients in a bowl and spread over fish.
Wrap in foil and bake in oven 190°C (375°F) for 30-45 minutes.
Serve hot.
Fish can be prepared in individual serves if wished.
Serve with salad.
Mild.
Serves 4.

Fish Kebabs

1 x 1 kg firm-fleshed fish
2 cloves garlic
125 g onions
150 mL yoghurt
salt to taste
½ teaspoon ginger
1 teaspoon chilli powder
2 teaspoons garam masala
melted butter for basting

Cut the fish into cubes.

Grind the garlic and add it to the bowl of water in which the fish is to be washed.
Wash and drain the fish cubes.
Grind the onions and mix with the yoghurt, salt and spices.
Marinate the fish in this mixture for 2 hours.
Drain and dry.
Thread the fish on to skewers and grill.
Brush with melted butter while grilling.
These can be served as a starter or as a main course on a bed of salad.
Serves 4-6.

Steamed Fish

1 × 500 g white fish
15 g almonds
2 bay leaves
½ green capsicum
2 teaspoons salt
15 mL mustard oil
300 mL yoghurt
½ teaspoon garam masala
½ teaspoon sugar

Clean and score the fish.
Blanch and toast almonds.
Mix all ingredients together and steam in a Chinese steamer or over a pan of boiling water until fish is done.
Serve with boiled potatoes or other vegetables.
Serves 2-4.

Fish Kofta Curry

1 kg white fish
3 medium onions
salt to taste
1 bay leaf
2 green chillies
a few sprigs of coriander or parsley
1 egg
2 tablespoons soft breadcrumbs
250 g ghee
1 clove garlic
1 teaspoon coriander
½ teaspoon cumin
1 teaspoon turmeric
1 teaspoon chilli

½ teaspoon ginger
250 g tomatoes
300 mL water

Cook the fish in a little water with half an onion, salt and the bay leaf till tender.
Cool and remove but keep the strained liquid.
Chop the green chillies and coriander leaves (or parsley).
Mash the fish and mix with the chopped green chillies and coriander leaves and the egg and crumbs.
Shape in balls the size of a plum and fry in ghee till brown.
Drain and keep aside.
Slice 1 onion finely.
Grind the rest of the onions and the garlic to a paste and add all the other spices.
Heat the ghee in a saucepan and fry the sliced onion until golden brown.
Add the chopped tomatoes and salt and cook covered till tomatoes are mixed into the gravy.
Add the liquid from the fish and 300 mL of water and bring to the boil; add the fish balls and simmer for 10 minutes.
Serve with rice.
Mild.
Serves 4-6.

Fish Kofta Curry

Bombay Fish Curry

Bombay Fish Curry

1 x 1 kg whole fish
60 g ghee, butter or oil
1 tablespoon chopped onion
1 clove garlic, finely minced
2 dried red chillies, cut lengthwise with seeds
removed
1 dessertspoon ground coriander
1 teaspoon ground turmeric
1 teaspoon ground mustard seed
¼ teaspoon ground chillies
½ teaspoon fresh ginger

coconut milk
1 teaspoon rice flour
salt
lemon juice

Lightly cook in the fat for 2 or 3 minutes the onions,
garlic, ginger, chillies and ground spices.
Add 300 mL of thin coconut milk in which a
teaspoon of rice flour has been mixed.
Add salt and lemon juice to taste.
Cook over a low heat until thick and add the fish.
When cooked add 2 tablespoons thick coconut milk.
The fish must not be stirred but the pan shaken every
now and again to prevent sticking.
Serves 4-6.

51

Roasted Spiced Fish

¼ green capsicum
bunch coriander leaves or parsley
1 teaspoon cumin
¼ teaspoon chilli
½ teaspoon ginger
½ teaspoon garlic salt
1 tablespoon garlic vinegar
1 × 500 g-1 kg whole fish
30 g butter

Chop the capsicum and coriander leaves.
Mix all the ingredients and salt with the vinegar.
Stuff the fish with this mixture, rubbing some on the outside as well.
Tie the fish with a string or wrap in tinfoil. (Butter fish before wrapping in foil.)
Put in greased baking dish and bake in a moderate oven.
If baking unwrapped, baste with butter and turn when red.
When fish is cooked pour off the gravy and thicken with a little flour, or the gravy may simply be left as it is.
Serve with salad.
Serves 4-8.

Coconut Spiced Fish

500 g white fish
3 tablespoons mustard oil
3 onions
½ green capsicum
300 mL thick coconut milk
2 teaspoons salt
juice of 1 lemon

Cut the fish across in slices and fry in part of the mustard oil.
In the rest of the heated mustard oil fry the chopped onions and green capsicum until the onions are a deep cream in colour. Add the fish, coconut milk and salt.
Cover and simmer till fish is cooked.
Remove from fire and add the lemon juice. Shake saucepan to mix.
Serves 4.

Prawn and Egg Curry

4 hard-boiled eggs cut in halves lengthwise
12 prawns (cooked)
60 g ghee
1½ tablespoons finely chopped onion
2 cloves garlic, finely chopped
2 fresh chillies, cut lengthwise
1 tablespoon curry powder
1 dessertspoon tomato paste
salt and lemon juice
thick coconut milk

Fry lightly for 3 or 4 minutes in ghee the onion, garlic and chillies, then add the curry powder and tomato paste.
Stir thoroughly and continue cooking slowly for 2 or 3 minutes longer.
Thin this mixture down into a thick gravy by gradually adding a little water.
Simmer gently.
Add salt and lemon juice to taste, and finally a little thick coconut milk.
Then add the eggs and prawns.
The gravy must be thick and cling to the eggs.
Serve with boiled rice.
Mild.
Serves 4.

Madras Prawn Curry

500 g prawns
1 tablespoon ghee
2 tablespoons finely chopped onion
2 cloves garlic
1 tablespoon curry powder
250 g fresh tomatoes
salt
lemon juice

For this recipe use cooked school prawns.
Make a sauce by putting into your pan a tablespoon of ghee, 2 tablespoons of finely chopped onion and 2 cloves of garlic, also finely chopped. Cook the onions and garlic until they begin to change colour, then add 1 tablespoon of curry powder. Stir well and let these ingredients fry for 3 or 4 minutes, then make into a thick sauce by adding 250 g of fresh tomatoes, skinned and finely chopped. Add salt and lemon juice to taste. Let the sauce simmer until the fat separates out, then add the prawns to the sauce. Let them just warm through. Do not boil or they will lose their flavour and fall to pieces.
Two tablespoons of thick coconut milk may be added before serving.
Crab, lobster and crayfish may be curried in the same way.
Serve with rice and Yoghurt and Cucumber Raita or Spiced Yoghurt.
Serves 4.

Roasted Spiced Fish

Fried Fish
(Bhoona Muchlee)

4 fillets of fish
1 beaten egg
1 level teaspoon turmeric
¼ level teaspoon ground chillies
1 small finely chopped onion
1 finely chopped clove garlic
juice of ½ lemon
salt to taste
oil for frying

Make a mixture of the egg, turmeric, chilli, onion, garlic, lemon juice and salt.
Marinate fish in this for ½ hour, turning from time to time.
Fry in hot fat over medium heat until golden brown.
Garnish with lemon and parsley.
Serve with rice or mashed potatoes and salad.
Mild.
Serves 4.

Fish Molee

A Molee is essentially a Southern Indian, Sri Lankan or Malay dish, the basis of which is coconut milk.
Vegetables, fish or meat can be used.

500 g fish fillets
60 g ghee
2 tablespoons chopped onion
1 teaspoon chopped garlic
4 green chillies, cut in half lengthwise
6 slices fresh green ginger
1 teaspoon turmeric
thick coconut milk
salt

Lightly fry the onions, garlic and ginger in the ghee.
Add the turmeric and green chillies.
Stir in sufficient coconut milk to make a gravy and salt.
Simmer for a few minutes.
Add the fish and cook slowly without stirring.
Mild.
Serves 4.

Fish Curry

500 g fish fillets
1 tablespoon of ground coriander
1 teaspoon of ground turmeric
1 teaspoon of ground cumin seed

Madras Prawn Curry (p. 52)

½ teaspoon of ground ginger
½ teaspoon of ground red chillies
½ teaspoon of ground fenugreek
mustard oil
2 small onions
3 cloves garlic
coconut milk
salt to taste

Blend the spices, ginger and chillies with a little tamarind juice or vinegar to make a curry paste.
Fry in 2 or 3 tablespoons of mustard oil, gingelly (sesame) oil, or ghee, 2 small onions and 2 or 3 cloves of garlic, sliced finely, then add the curry paste and cook for another 5 minutes. Add sufficient coconut milk to make a thick gravy.
Salt to taste.
Add whatever kind of fish you have to the sauce, keep the pan uncovered, and simmer gently for 10-15 minutes or until the fish is cooked.
Shake the pan occasionally to prevent the fish sticking.
Mild.
Serves 4.

Prawns in Garlic and Chilli Sauce

1 kg green king prawns, shelled
3 cloves garlic, crushed
2 teaspoons sugar
1 chicken stock cube
1 teaspoon soy sauce
½ teaspoon sesame oil
2 tablespoons cornflour
salt and pepper
5 tablespoons cooking oil
2 teaspoons oyster sauce (optional)
2 tablespoons water
1 tablespoon ginger wine
1 tablespoon chilli sauce
1 tablespoon tomato sauce
1 large onion, cubed
1 capsicum, diced
2 shallots, chopped

Put prawns in a bowl and add garlic, sugar, chicken stock cube, soy sauce, sesame oil, 1 tablespoon of the cornflour and salt and pepper to taste. Mix well and allow to stand for 10 minutes.
In a frying pan, heat 4 tablespoons of the oil, add prawns and fry for 5 minutes, then remove to a plate.
In a bowl, mix oyster sauce (optional), remaining 1 tablespoon cornflour mixed to a paste with 2 tablespoons water, ginger wine, chilli sauce and tomato sauce to form a paste. Set aside.
In a large pan, heat remaining 1 tablespoon oil, add

onion and fry for 2 minutes, then add capsicum and stir.
Add fried prawns to pan, then the mixed sauce paste. Stir gently. Continue to fry for 5 minutes until the sauce is thick.
Remove from heat and sprinkle with chopped shallots.
Transfer to a flat plate and serve hot with rice.
Serves 6-8.

Prawn and Cucumber Curry

750g large prawns, shelled, but with tails intact
½ teaspoon paprika or chilli powder (optional)
1 tablespoon curry powder
pinch turmeric
thin slice ginger, cut into strips
1 clove garlic, crushed
salt
3 tablespoons cooking oil
1 large onion, sliced finely
1 cup canned coconut milk or 30g coconut cream mixed with 1 cup of water
1 cucumber, peeled, seeded and diced
2 fresh green chillies, halved
1 tablespoon vinegar

In a bowl, mix prawns, paprika or chilli powder (optional), curry powder, turmeric, ginger, garlic and salt to taste and allow to stand for 5 minutes. Heat oil in a frying pan, fry onion until golden brown.
Add seasoned prawns and fry, stirring for 10 minutes.
Add cream of coconut and cucumber, mix well and bring to the boil.
Add green chillies and vinegar, boil for 2 seconds only, stir and remove from heat.
Serve hot with rice or bread.
Serves 4.

Prawns in Coconut

500g medium green prawns, shelled
1 teaspoon vinegar
salt and pepper
pinch turmeric
3 tablespoons cooking oil
¼ teaspoon mustard seed
1 teaspoon uncooked rice
1 small onion, chopped
1 clove garlic, chopped
thin slice ginger, chopped
2 fresh green chillies, halved or ½ capsicum, chopped
2 curry leaves
4 tablespoons desiccated coconut

Fish Molee (p. 55)

Put prawns in a bowl, add vinegar, salt and pepper to taste, and turmeric. Mix well and allow to stand for 15 minutes.
In a frying pan, heat cooking oil, add mustard seed and fry for 2 seconds only, then add rice and fry until it bubbles.
Add onions and fry until golden brown. Add garlic and ginger and fry for 2 minutes, stirring. Add seasoned prawns, fry for 10 minutes, stirring constantly, then add chillies, curry leaves and desiccated coconut. Continue to cook and stir for 5 minutes and remove from heat.
Serve with fluffy rice and vegetables.
Serves 4.

Prawns, Pork and Bamboo Shoots Fried in Sauce

250g medium green prawns, shelled
250g pork meat, cut into 25mm cubes
salt and pepper
½ teaspoon sugar
2 chicken stock cubes
1 teaspoon soy sauce
½ teaspoon sesame oil
2 tablespoons cooking oil
1 tablespoon Worcestershire sauce
3 tablespoons water
1 teaspoon black bean sauce
2 tablespoons cornflour
185g bamboo shoots, diced
1 capsicum, diced
1 cucumber, peeled, seeded and diced
Garnish: 1 stalk celery, diced
2 tablespoons green peas, cooked

In a bowl, mix prawns, pork cubes, salt and pepper to taste, sugar, chicken stock cubes, soy sauce and sesame oil and allow to stand for 5 minutes. Remove pork to another bowl.
In a frying pan, heat oil, add seasoned prawns and fry for 5 minutes, stirring gently all the time. Remove prawns and put aside.
Add seasoned pork to pan and fry on all sides until cooked. Remove pork and put aside. Leave the remaining oil in the pan for later use.
In a bowl, mix Worcestershire sauce, water, black bean sauce and cornflour to form a paste.
Reheat oil in which prawns and pork were cooked and add sauce mixture, bamboo shoots, capsicum and cucumber. Mix well, bring to the boil, and simmer until sauce thickens.
Reduce heat and add fried prawns and pork. Mix well and remove to a serving dish.
Garnish with celery and cooked peas.
Serves 4.

VEGETABLES
AND EGGS

Many Indian people are vegetarian for religious reasons. As a result, great attention has been paid to the cooking of vegetables in Indian cuisine. The recipes in this section vary from very simple dishes (ideal as accompaniments to meat, fish or chicken curries) to more complicated and filling dishes (which can be served as meals in themselves with bread or rice, and perhaps salad and chutney).

You may like to experiment with alternative combinations of any vegetables in season which are plentiful, cheap and of good quality. In the mixed vegetable dishes, particularly, you should feel free to add any vegetables you have to hand — or to leave out any you do not.

If you intend to freeze a vegetable curry, ensure that you undercook it slightly — then freeze and reheat as required.

Though eggs are widely eaten in India by vegetarians and non-vegetarians alike, some orthodox vegetarians (known as vegans) avoid them. The Parsees, of Persian origin, who live on the west coast of India have a fondness for eggs, and omelettes in particular play an important part in their cuisine.

Eggs can be cooked in very elaborate ways but they are also an excellent basis for very simple, quickly-cooked yet substantial dishes. As they can be stored easily they are a very good stand-by when unexpected guests arrive.

Chitchkee (Vegetable Curry)

500 g mixed raw vegetables (peas, carrots, beans, turnip, cauliflower or potatoes)
2 tablespoons ghee
1 onion sliced
2 cloves garlic, sliced
250 g chopped tomatoes
2 tablespoons curry powder
water or stock
salt to taste
squeeze of lemon juice

Fry the onion, garlic and curry powder in the ghee.
Mix in the tomatoes and add sufficient water or stock to make a gravy.
Add the vegetables and salt.
Simmer for about 20 minutes or until the vegetables are cooked.
Add a squeeze of lemon juice.
Serve with chapatis or pooris.
Mild to medium.
Serves 4.

Chitchkee (Vegetable Curry)

59

Aubergine and Green Capsicum Curry

1 large onion
500 g aubergines
250 g tomatoes
250 g green capsicum
90 g ghee
1 teaspoon turmeric
¼ teaspoon ginger powder
salt to taste
1 teaspoon garam masala

Slice onion finely.
Wash aubergines, tomatoes and green capsicum.
Cut aubergines into 2-inch pieces and tomatoes into quarters.
Slice green capsicum.
Heat the ghee and fry the onions till pale golden.
Add the aubergines, turmeric, ginger and salt and fry for 5 minutes.
Then add the tomatoes and green capsicum and after stirring well cover and cook for 15 minutes or till the aubergines are tender.
Sprinkle the garam masala over the curry and keep over a very low heat for another 2 minutes.
Serve with boiled rice, chapatis or pooris.
Mild.
Serves 6-8.

French Beans Bhujia

A 'Bhujia' is a dry vegetable curry.

750 g French beans
1 onion
60 g ghee
1 teaspoon turmeric
½ teaspoon chilli (optional)
salt to taste
½ teaspoon garam masala

Wash and cut the beans into small pieces.
Chop onion.
Heat the ghee and fry the onion lightly.
Add the beans, turmeric, chilli and salt and fry for 3 minutes.
Sprinkle over garam masala, cover and cook over a very low heat for about 15 minutes or till the beans are soft.
Serve as an accompaniment.
Mild.
Serves 4-6.

Leek Bhujia

1 kg leeks
salt to taste
60 g ghee
½ teaspoon cumin seed

French Beans Bhujia

1 teaspoon turmeric
½ teaspoon ginger powder
½ teaspoon garam masala

Wash leeks and slice thinly. Soak in salted water,
wash again and drain.
Heat the ghee and add the cumin seeds. Fry for a few
seconds then add the leeks, turmeric, ginger and salt.
Fry for 3 or 4 minutes; cover and cook over gentle
heat till leeks are tender.
Sprinkle with garam masala and serve hot as an
accompaniment.
Mild.
Serves 6-8.

Cabbage and Potato Curry

1 large cabbage
1 tablespoon rice
3 potatoes
2 onions
½ green capsicum or 2 green chillies
45 g ghee

½ teaspoon garam masala
¼ teaspoon ginger
¼ teaspoon turmeric
¼ teaspoon chilli
½ teaspoon sugar
1 teaspoon salt
300 mL hot water

Slice and steam the cabbage.
Soak the rice in cold water for 30 minutes.
Boil the potatoes whole then cut into 8 pieces each.
Slice the onions and green capsicum.
Heat the ghee and fry the potatoes.
Drain and keep aside.
Fry the onions, garam masala and drained rice for a
minute, then add the ginger, turmeric and chilli.
Brown and add 300 mL hot water and simmer for
about 10 minutes or till the rice is cooked.
Put in the cabbage, potatoes and sliced green
capsicum.
Stir and add sugar and salt.
Simmer till nearly all the liquid has evaporated.
Serve hot.
Mild.
Serves 6-8.

Mushroom Bhujia

375 g mushrooms
2 large onions
125 g ghee
1 teaspoon turmeric
1 teaspoon chilli
1 clove garlic, chopped
salt to taste

Wash and dry the mushrooms.
If large cut into pieces.
Slice onions finely.
Heat the ghee and fry the onions till they are soft.
Add the turmeric, chilli and the garlic (chopped fine) and fry for 1 minute.
Add mushrooms and salt and cook over gentle heat for a few minutes till mushrooms are ready.
Mild.
Serves 4-6.

Okra (Ladies' Fingers) Bhujia

500 g okra
90 g ghee
1 medium onion
1 teaspoon turmeric
salt to taste
black pepper

Wash and dry okra and cut into small pieces.
Heat the ghee and fry the sliced onion till pale golden.
Add the okra and the turmeric, fry for 1 minute and add the salt and pepper.
Cook over a very low heat for about 20 minutes or till ready.
Serve as an accompaniment.
Mild.
Serves 4-6.

Cauliflower in Yoghurt

1 large cauliflower
3 onions
2 cloves garlic
½ teaspoon ginger
300 mL yoghurt
1 teaspoon sugar
1 teaspoon salt
45 g ghee
1 teaspoon garam masala
150 mL hot water

Divide the cauliflower into flowerettes.
Slice 1½ onions finely.
Mince the other 1½ onions with garlic and ginger.
Put the yoghurt in a bowl, add the minced ingredients, sugar and salt and beat with a whisk.
Marinate the cauliflower in the yoghurt for 2 hours, making sure that the yoghurt covers the flowerettes.
Heat the ghee and fry the onions till golden.
Add the cauliflower, all the yoghurt and 150 mL hot water.
Simmer for 15 minutes or till cauliflower is tender.
Sprinkle with garam masala.
Mild.
Serves 6-8.

Stuffed Tomatoes

6 medium sized firm tomatoes
1 small onion
1 clove garlic
1 tablespoon ghee
1 teaspoon curry powder or paste
1 minced raw chicken breast (or other meat may be used)
salt to taste

Remove a slice from each tomato to form a lid, scoop out some of the inside and reserve.
Finely mince onion and garlic and fry in ghee until soft.
Add chicken and curry powder and cook gently for 6 minutes.
Add tomato pulp and salt.
Place mixture into tomato cases, and bake in oven about 30 minutes or until tomato case is cooked but still retains its shape.
Serve as a starter or as a main meal with rice and salad.
Mild.
Serves 6.

Alu Tari (Potato Curry)

500 g potatoes
250 g tomatoes
60 g ghee
1 teaspoon turmeric
1 teaspoon cumin seed
salt to taste
1 teaspoon chilli

Peel and dice the potatoes.
Chop the tomatoes.
Melt the ghee and add the potatoes, turmeric, cumin

Cauliflower in Yoghurt

Alu Tari (Potato Curry) (p. 62)

and salt and fry for 5 minutes.
Add the tomatoes and chilli powder and fry for 2 or 3 minutes.
Add enough hot water to cover the potatoes.
Bring to the boil and simmer about 15 minutes or till tender.
There should be plenty of gravy.
Mild.
Serves 4-6.

Spinach and Potato Curry

1 kg spinach
250 g potatoes (new if available)
60 g ghee
1 large onion, sliced
1 teaspoon cumin seed
2 green chillies
½ teaspoon ginger powder
salt to taste
125 mL water

Stuffed Tomatoes (p. 62)

Wash the spinach.
Peel or scrape the potatoes and cut into quarters.
Heat the ghee and fry the onion till golden.
Add the potatoes, cumin, chopped green chillies, ginger and water, and cook for 5 minutes, stirring all the time.
Add the spinach and cover the pan for 2 minutes.
Add the salt and cook uncovered till the water has evaporated.
Cover and cook over very gentle heat for 20 minutes or till ready.
Mild.
Serves 6-8.

Zucchini and Potatoes

4 tablespoons cooking oil
1 onion, chopped finely
1 clove garlic, chopped
4 potatoes, peeled, boiled and cut into 25 mm cubes
1 teaspoon paprika
salt and pepper
¼ teaspoon each turmeric, cumin, cinnamon, clove powder and cardamom powder

500g zucchini, sliced thinly lengthways, then into
   pieces 25 mm long
1 tomato, diced
1 teaspoon vinegar or lemon juice (optional)
green part of 2 shallots, chopped

Heat oil in a deep frying pan. Add onions and fry
until golden brown.
Add garlic, potatoes, paprika, salt and pepper to taste,
turmeric, cumin, cinnamon and clove and cardamom
powders and fry for 15 minutes stirring frequently.
Add zucchini and continue to fry, stirring, for 10
minutes.
Add tomatoes, vinegar (optional) and shallots.
Continue frying for 5 minutes, stirring frequently to
prevent burning, then remove to a serving dish.
Serve hot with rice or bread.
Serves 6.

Cabbage in Coconut

2 tablespoons cooking oil
½ teaspoon mustard seed
1 large onion, chopped
1 clove garlic, crushed (optional)
¼ teaspoon cumin
¼ teaspoon turmeric
10 cabbage leaves, washed, drained and shredded
2 fresh green chillies, chopped coarsely
2 curry leaves
2 tablespoons desiccated coconut
salt

Heat oil in a frying pan on moderate heat, add
mustard seed and fry for 2 seconds only, then add
onions and fry until golden brown.
Add garlic (optional), cumin, turmeric, shredded
cabbage, chillies, curry leaves, desiccated coconut and
salt to taste and mix well. Cover and continue
cooking for 5 minutes.
Remove lid and continue frying, stirring constantly
for 10 minutes or until cabbage is cooked and water
has been absorbed.
Serve hot with rice and curry.
Serves 4.

Tomato, Egg and Coconut

2 tablespoons cooking oil
¼ teaspoon mustard seed
1 onion, minced
thin slice ginger, minced
¼ teaspoon turmeric
4 green tomatoes, minced
¼ teaspoon pepper

salt
2 eggs, beaten
4 tablespoons desiccated coconut
3 shallots, minced

Heat oil in frying pan on moderate heat, add mustard
seed, fry for 5 seconds only, then add onion, ginger
and turmeric and fry for 2 minutes. Add tomatoes,
pepper and salt to taste, stir well, then add beaten
eggs. Cook, stirring, for 5 minutes.
Add desiccated coconut and spring onions. Continue
to fry for 5 minutes, then remove from heat. Serve
with rice.
Serves 4.

Cabbage and Carrot Bhujia

1 cabbage
350g carrots
½-1 fresh hot green chilli
4 tablespoons oil
1 tablespoon whole black mustard seeds
1 dried red chilli
1¼ teaspoons salt
½ teaspoon sugar
4 tablespoons chopped fresh green coriander
1 tablespoon lemon juice

Core and shred cabbage. Peel carrots and grate
coarsely. Cut green chilli into long thin strips.
Heat oil in wide casserole dish over medium heat.
When hot put in mustard seeds and fry for a few
seconds only. Add dried red chilli and stir. The chilli
will turn dark red very quickly.
Add cabbage, carrots and green chilli. Lower heat and
stir-fry the vegetables for about 30 seconds. Add salt,
sugar and green coriander. Stir fry for another five
minutes until vegetables are just done making sure
that they are still crisp. Add the lemon juice and stir.
Remove the dark red chilli before serving.
Mild to Medium.
Serves 4-6.

Egg Curry

4 to 6 eggs
2 onions
2 cloves garlic
250g tomatoes

Madras Egg Curry (p. 69)

66

120g ghee
1 teaspoon ginger
2 teaspoons coriander
1 teaspoon chilli
1 teaspoon garam masala
1 teaspoon turmeric
1 teaspoon cumin
1 teaspoon paprika
salt to taste

Hard-boil the eggs and when cold cut into halves. Slice 1 onion and grind the other onion and the garlic to a paste. Chop the tomatoes.
Heat the ghee and fry the sliced onion to a golden brown. Take pan off the heat and add the paste and all the other spices and salt. Fry on a low heat for 5 minutes.
Add the tomatoes, cover and simmer till the gravy is thick. Add the eggs and simmer for 5 minutes.
Serves 2-3.

Madras Egg Curry

6 eggs
60g ghee
2 tablespoons chopped onions
1 clove garlic
1 tablespoon curry powder
250g fresh tomatoes
salt and lemon juice to taste

Hard-boil eggs, then cut in halves lengthwise.
In 50g ghee fry lightly for 2 or 3 minutes chopped onions and clove of garlic, finely sliced. Add 1 tablespoon of curry powder.
Stir thoroughly, and continue the frying for 2 or 3 minutes longer.
Add the tomatoes, finely chopped, and sufficient water to form a thickish gravy.
Add salt and lemon juice to taste and simmer for 5 to 10 minutes. Add the eggs and warm through.
Serve with boiled rice.
Mild.
Serves 2-3.

Baked Spiced Eggs

2 large onions
2 cloves garlic
1 small bunch fresh coriander or watercress
¼ green capsicum
60g ghee
4 eggs
1 tablespoon vinegar or Worcestershire sauce

Indian Savoury Omelet

1 teaspoon sugar
½ teaspoon cumin powder
½ teaspoon salt

Thinly slice onions. Finely chop garlic, coriander or watercress and green capsicum.
Mix the vinegar or Worcestershire sauce with the sugar. Fry the onions till almond coloured.
Add the garlic, green capsicum and coriander or watercress to the onions. Fry for 3 minutes, stirring all the time.
Beat the eggs and add to the onions in the saucepan. Add cumin powder.
Remove from the heat and pour in vinegar or Worcestershire sauce and salt. Stir the mixture well. Pour into an ovenproof dish and put in preheated oven 200°C (400°F) to set. This should take just over 30 minutes.
Serves 2-4.

Indian Savoury Omelet

2 eggs
1 small onion finely minced
1 green chilli finely minced
pepper and salt to taste
pinch of minced mint or mixed herbs
1 dessertspoon ghee

Beat the two eggs well and add 1 small onion and 1 green chilli very finely minced.
Add pepper and salt to taste, and if liked, a pinch of finely minced mint or mixed herbs. Beat all together for a minute or two.
Melt a dessertspoon of ghee in an omelet pan. Pour in the mixture and cook slowly until the omelet is firm underneath. Then either fold the omelet in half and cook until done, or turn the omelet right over and cook on the other side.
Serve as a starter or as a main course with boiled rice and lentils or Cottage Cheese Salad.
Mild.
Serves 2.

Egg Curry with Potatoes

3 tablespoons cooking oil
¼ teaspoon mustard seeds
2 large onions, chopped
2 cloves garlic, chopped
thin slice ginger, chopped or pounded
1 large ripe tomato, chopped
½ teaspoon chilli powder
3½ tablespoons coriander or curry powder
¼ teaspoon white pepper
¼ teaspoon each cumin, aniseed, turmeric,
    cinnamon, clove powder, cardamom powder

2 fresh green chillies, halved
1 tablespoon tomato paste
salt
4 tablespoons water
4 large potatoes, peeled and halved
8 hard-boiled eggs, shelled
125 g coconut cream mixed with 1 cup water
1 teaspoon vinegar or lemon juice

Heat oil in a pan, add mustard seed, fry for 10
seconds only then add onions and fry until golden
brown.
Add garlic, ginger and tomato and continue to fry for
10 minutes, stirring occasionally. Pour into a
saucepan.
In a bowl, mix chilli powder, coriander, pepper,
cumin, aniseed, turmeric, cinnamon, clove powder,
cardamom powder, chillies, tomato paste, salt to taste
and water to make a paste.
Add paste to the saucepan, mix well. Fry for 5
minutes, add potatoes and cook on moderate heat
until potatoes are tender.
Add hard-boiled eggs and coconut cream, stir well,
then add vinegar and bring to the boil. Remove from
heat and serve with rice and vegetables.
Serves 8.

Omelet (Parsee recipe)

4 eggs
2 egg yolks
1 medium-sized onion, finely chopped
90 g butter
2 tablespoons chopped coriander leaves
1 green chilli, seeded and finely chopped
1 clove of garlic, crushed
pinch of ground ginger
salt
2 tablespoons tamarind juice

Fry the onions to a pale gold in the butter in a large
omelet pan.
Beat the eggs and yolks together slightly and stir in
the coriander, chilli, garlic, ginger and a pinch of salt
and mix in tamarind juice.
Pour the egg mixture over the onions in the pan, stir
mixture and tip pan until it is set, but do not
overcook.
Slide omelet from the pan on to a hot flat dish and
serve at once, either plain, or with boiled rice, lentils
and a salad.
Mild.
Serves 4.

A selection of accompaniments

ACCOMPANIMENTS

Side dishes are an essential part of an Indian meal. Their flavours and textures add variety, refresh the palate, and provide a contrast to curries. Salads, sambals (imaginative side-dishes of fruit, vegetables or nuts) and raitas (grated vegetables with yoghurt) are traditional accompaniments.

Almost any vegetables can be used to make an interesting salad. Fresh and canned fruits, such as pineapple, mango and melon, also make delicious side dishes. (See 'Chutneys, Pickles and Sauces' for other ideas.) Many Indian chutneys are not cooked, but are delicious, cool combinations of fresh vegetables and fruits.

Sambals — presented in small, separate dishes — are popular and easy accompaniments to serve with the main course. The variety is endless, and as unrestricted as the imagination and individual taste of the cook.

The following ideas will provide an indication of the range of sambals. Diced apples or bananas and desiccated coconut can be mixed with finely chopped onion and chillies. Sprinkle with salt and lemon juice. Chopped cucumber or tomato can be mixed with garlic, onion, lemon juice and salt, sprinkled with coconut. Yoghurt can be combined with chopped tomato, onion, chillies and salt to taste. Various nuts, fried onion rings, pickles, chutneys and fresh fruits are also served.

Raitas, usually consisting of grated vegetables with a base of yoghurt, are the most common accompaniment to curries and are eaten in larger quantities than chutneys or pickles. Like salads, they are easy and quick to make, and have a high protein content.

Yoghurt with Cucumber and Mint

570 mL yoghurt
1 cucumber, peeled and coarsely grated
2 tablespoons finely chopped fresh mint
½ teaspoon ground, roasted cumin seeds
¼ teaspoon cayenne pepper
1 teaspoon salt
freshly ground black pepper

Put yoghurt in bowl and beat lightly with fork or whisk until smooth and creamy. Add all other ingredients and mix well. Cover and refrigerate until ready to eat.
Serves 6.

Pumpkin and Mustard Salad (p. 74)

Yoghurt with Walnuts and Fresh Coriander

570 mL yoghurt
2 tablespoons finely chopped fresh coriander
½ fresh green chilli, finely chopped
salt to taste
freshly ground black pepper
1 shallot, finely sliced
60 g shelled walnuts broken roughly into small pieces

Put yoghurt in bowl. Beat lightly with a fork or whisk to a smooth, creamy liquid. Add all the other ingredients and mix well.
Serves 6.

Grilled Aubergine

500 g aubergines
a little olive oil
1 medium onion
2 green chillies
30 g ghee
½ teaspoon cumin seed
salt to taste

Rub the aubergines with oil and grill until the skin is scorched and brown.
Cool and remove the skin.
Mash the pulp.
Chop the onion and the chillies.
Heat the ghee and fry the onions for a few minutes till lightly browned.
Add the cumin seed, aubergine pulp and chopped chillies.
Fry for 3 minutes.
Add salt, stir and remove from heat.
Serves 4-6.

Cottage Cheese Salad

500 g cottage cheese
250 g onions
1 teaspoon salt
2 tablespoons desiccated coconut
4 tablespoons hot milk
½ green capsicum
12 sprigs green coriander or watercress leaves
juice of 2 lemons
¼ teaspoon freshly ground pepper

Peel and slice onions thinly crosswise.
Sprinkle with ½ teaspoon salt and rub in with hands.

Let stand for 30 minutes, then pour cold water over and drain well.
Soak the coconut in hot milk and let stand for 30 minutes.
Chop the green pepper and coriander or watercress leaves coarsely.
Mix everything together and stir well.
Set aside for 30 minutes after mixing.
Serve cold.
Serves 4-6.

Pumpkin and Mustard Salad

250 g pumpkin
¼ green capsicum
½ teaspoon dry mustard
¼ teaspoon ginger
½ teaspoon cumin
½ teaspoon salt
150 mL yoghurt

Peel and slice pumpkin.
Chop green capsicum very fine.
Boil pumpkin, drain and keep warm.
Mix mustard, ginger, cumin, salt and green pepper into the yoghurt.
Add the pumpkin.
Mix well and serve.
White marrow may be used instead of pumpkin. This dish can be varied by using sliced bananas, tomatoes, cucumbers, boiled cauliflower sprigs or boiled slices of cabbage. Adjust quantity of mustard to taste.
This makes an excellent accompaniment for spicy curries.
Serves 4-6.

Vegetable Salad

6 lettuce leaves, shredded
1 cucumber, peeled and diced
2 tomatoes, cut into wedges
2 boiled potatoes, cut into 25 mm cubes
2 hard-boiled eggs, sliced thickly
1 carrot, scraped, cut into thin rings and boiled or left raw and shredded

Sauce
2 tablespoons crunchy peanut butter
½ teaspoon brown sugar
1 tablespoon lime juice
4 tablespoons chilli sauce
1 teaspoon soy sauce
salt

Mix salad ingredients gently in a salad bowl, preferably glass as this looks decorative on the table, or arrange on an open platter. Keep in the refrigerator, covered, until required.
Mix sauce ingredients in a bowl (the mixture should be thick) and put aside.
To serve, pour sauce over vegetable salad or serve separately and dip vegetables in the sauce.
Serve with rice as a side dish.
Serve 4-6.

Cucumber and Pineapple Salad

1 large cucumber, peeled and sliced or diced
1 cup canned pineapple cubes with syrup or canned crushed pineapple with syrup or fresh pineapple cubes
1 small onion, minced
1 fresh green chilli or ½ capsicum, minced coarsely
pinch salt

In a glass salad bowl combine cucumber, pineapple cubes with syrup, minced onion, green chillies and salt.
Chill and serve with rice and curry or Pilau.
Serves 4-6.

Cucumber, Onion and Celery Salad

1 large cucumber, peeled and sliced
1 large onion, sliced finely
3 stalks celery, minced or chopped finely
1 tablespoon chilli sauce or 2 tablespoons tomato sauce

Arrange cucumber rings and onion on a platter or in a bowl and sprinkle minced celery over. Keep in the refrigerator until required.
When serving, pour chilli sauce or tomato sauce over salad.
Serve with Pilau or any curry.
Serves 4-6.

Spiced Yoghurt

1½ tablespoons oil
¼ teaspoon mustard seed
pinch fenugreek

1 small onion, chopped finely
2 cloves garlic, chopped finely
2 dry red chillies, cut into 15 mm pieces
¼ teaspoon cumin
1 fresh green chilli, chopped finely
3 curry leaves
salt
2 cups natural yoghurt, beaten well

Heat oil in a frying pan, add mustard seed and fry for 2 seconds only. Add fenugreek, then onions and fry until golden brown.
Lower heat, then add garlic, dry chillies, cumin, green chilli, curry leaves and salt to taste. Stir for 5 seconds and remove pan from heat.
Add beaten yoghurt, mix well and pour into a bowl.
Do not boil yoghurt.
Chill in refrigerator.
Serve cold with plain rice, saffron rice or with any curry.
Serves 4-6.

Banana and Coconut Salad

bananas
desiccated coconut
lemon juice (optional)

Peel required number of bananas (allow half a small banana per person), and slice thinly.
Sprinkle desiccated coconut over banana and gently mix until all slices are well covered with coconut.
Serve within an hour of cutting banana or it may brown or, if liked, sprinkle banana rings with lemon juice before rolling in coconut, to stop them browning.
Serve with any curry.

Sambal Dressing

In a little ghee or oil fry the following ingredients lightly on a slow heat until the onions are cooked but not browned:—

1 large onion finely minced
1 clove of garlic finely minced
2 green chillies finely minced
½ teaspoon ground ginger
½ teaspoon ground cumin seed
1 teaspoon ground turmeric
1 pinch ground red chillies

Prawn Sambal

Into the sambal dressing blend chopped, cooked prawns, a dessertspoon of thick coconut milk and a heaped dessertspoon of desiccated coconut. Add salt and lemon juice to taste.
This sambal can be served either hot or cold and is usually garnished with sliced hard-boiled eggs.

Tomato Sambal

This is a blend of finely sliced fresh tomatoes and onions, 1 or 2 green chillies chopped finely, lemon juice, pepper and salt to taste. When served, sprinkle with desiccated or freshly grated coconut.

Potato Sambal

Lightly mix cooked, diced potato with chopped green chillies and a pinch of red chilli powder. Add ½ teaspoon sliced spring onions or very finely chopped onion and a sprinkling of olive oil. Add salt and lemon juice to taste.
Serve with pooris.

Sambal of Mixed Vegetables

Using a combination of cooked, diced carrots, peas, beans, turnips and potatoes, proceed as for Tomato Sambal.

Egg Sambal

Cut hard-boiled eggs in halves lengthwise and mix lightly with very finely chopped onion, fresh green or pickled chillies, oil, lemon juice and salt to taste.
When served sprinkle with desiccated or fresh grated coconut.
This dish makes a good starter.

Sambal Sauce

This creamy but piquant sauce is made with coconut milk to which is added finely chopped onion, a little garlic and a fairly generous pinch of ground red chillies.

Butter or Haricot Bean Sambal

Sprinkle cooked butter beans or haricot beans with ground red chillies or fresh or pickled chillies. Add salt and lemon juice to taste or toss ingredients in Sambal Sauce.

Banana Sambal

Thinly slice firm, green bananas and sprinkle with ground red chillies or finely chopped fresh or pickled chillies. Add salt and lemon juice to taste. As an alternative, blend the sliced bananas with Sambal Sauce.

Apple Sambal

Cut sour, green apples into small dice and sprinkle with ground red chillies and salt and lemon juice to taste. Again, as an alternative, blend with Sambal Sauce.

Samosas

Pastry:
500 g plain flour
½ teaspoon baking powder
1 teaspoon salt
30 g ghee
4 tablespoons yoghurt

Filling:
60 g ghee
1 small onion
500 g boiled potatoes
2 green chillies

*Prawn Sambal (p. 75) and
Butter or Haricot Bean Sambal*

salt to taste
1 teaspoon garam masala
oil for deep frying

To make the pastry, sieve the flour, baking powder and salt into a bowl.
Add the 30 g melted butter or ghee and the yoghurt and make into a pliable dough. Knead thoroughly till dough is smooth.
To make filling, heat the 60 g ghee and fry the chopped onion for 2 minutes.
Add the potatoes and chillies cut into small pieces and fry for 5 minutes. Add salt and garam masala and mix thoroughly.
Remove from heat and cool.
Knead dough again. Take small walnut-size pieces of the dough and make into round balls. Flatten and roll out on a floured board, making thin rounds the size of a saucer.
Cut the rounds in half. Make into a cone, seal with water and fill with the potato mixture. Wet open edges with water and press together. When all the samosas are ready, fry in deep fat or oil till crisp and golden.
Makes 15-20.

Samosas with Meat

1 onion
2 cloves garlic
30 g ghee
375 g mince meat
2 teaspoons coriander
½ teaspoon ginger
½ teaspoon chilli
1 teaspoon garam masala
salt to taste

Chop the onion and garlic very finely.
Heat the ghee and fry the onion and garlic till golden.
Add the mince, spices and salt and fry for 5 minutes.
Cover and cook over gentle heat for about 30 minutes or till the meat is cooked.
If the mixture dries out before the meat is done add a little water.
Cool and fill samosas as in the preceding recipe.
Makes 15-20.

Samosas with Potatoes and Peas

1 onion
60 g ghee
250 g boiled diced potatoes
250 g peas

2 green chillies, chopped
salt to taste
1 teaspoon garam masala

Fry the chopped onion in the ghee for 2 minutes.
Add the potatoes, peas and chillies and fry for 5
minutes.
Add salt and garam masala.
Remove from heat and cool.
Fill samosas as in the first recipe.
Makes 15-20.

Pakoras

Basic Batter:
250 g besan (lentil flour)
¼ teaspoon baking powder
½ teaspoon turmeric
vegetables (see method)
1 teaspoon coriander powder
½ teaspoon chilli powder
salt to taste
water

Sieve besan, baking powder, turmeric, coriander,
chilli and salt into a bowl.
Gradually add water and beat to a thick batter.
To make pakoras, 250 g onions may be chopped and
added to the batter and dropped in teaspoonfuls into
hot fat or oil and deep fried till crisp.
Potatoes cut in thin slices, aubergines cut into 6 mm
rounds, cauliflower flowerettes and spinach leaves
may be dipped in batter and fried as above.

Prawn Fritters

500 g small cooked prawns, shelled
½ cup rice flour
½ cup self-raising flour
1 tablespoon cornflour
1 teaspoon baking powder
½ cup semolina flour
½ cup besan
1 large onion, chopped finely
thin slice ginger, chopped finely
½ capsicum, chopped finely
leaves of 3 shallots, chopped
¼ teaspoon turmeric
¼ teaspoon cumin
salt and pepper
¼ teaspoon chilli powder (optional)
2 eggs, beaten
water as required for mixing
1 cup cooking oil

Put prawns in a bowl. Add rice flour, self-raising
flour, cornflour, baking powder, semolina flour,

besan, onion, ginger, capsicum, shallot leaves,
turmeric, cumin, salt and pepper to taste, chilli
powder (optional) and beaten eggs.
Mix well and add sufficient water to make a thick
paste. Allow to stand for 15 minutes.
Heat cooking oil in a frying pan over moderate heat.
Drop one tablespoon of batter at a time into the oil
and fry until golden brown on both sides. Drain well
and arrange on a plate.
Serve hot with tomato sauce or chilli sauce as a dip.
Makes 15-20.

Cheese and Potato Fritters

1 cup self-raising flour
1 cup grated cheese
1 large onion, chopped
500 g potatoes
2 eggs, beaten well
1 teaspoon baking powder
salt and pepper
1 teaspoon paprika
½ cup evaporated milk
2 cups cooking oil

In a bowl, mix self-raising flour, grated cheese,
potatoes, beaten eggs, baking powder, salt and pepper
to taste, paprika and milk. Mix well to make a thick
batter and allow to stand for 5 minutes.
Heat oil in a frying pan over moderate heat. Drop
batter, one tablespoon at a time, into the oil, and fry
fritters on both sides until golden brown.
Drain well and serve hot with chilli sauce or
chutneys.
Makes 15-20.

Vegetable and Potato Fritters (Bhajis)

2 cups besan
½ cup self-raising flour
2 tablespoons cornflour
3 tablespoons rice flour
1 teaspoon baking powder
1 large potato, shredded
1 large carrot, shredded
1 large onion, chopped
¼ teaspoon chilli powder
¼ teaspoon cumin
¼ teaspoon turmeric
salt
3 shallots, chopped finely

Samosas with Meat and Potato and
Pea Fillings (p. 77)

1 cup water (or more if needed)
1 teaspoon lemon juice
1½ cups cooking oil

In a mixing bowl, mix besan, self-raising flour, cornflour, rice flour, baking powder, potato, carrot, onion, chilli, cumin, turmeric, salt to taste, chopped shallots, water, lemon juice, and 1 tablespoon of the oil. Mix well to form a thick batter, and allow to stand for 5 minutes.

Heat remaining oil in a frying pan over moderate heat. Drop batter, 1 tablespoon at a time, into the oil, and fry fritters on both sides until golden brown. Drain well and serve hot with chutneys, chilli sauce or tomato sauce.

Makes 20.

Pakoras (p. 78)

Some of the basic ingredients for
chutneys, pickles and sauces

CHUTNEYS, PICKLES AND SAUCES

Chutneys, pickles and sauces are designed as curry accompaniments and form an important part of an Indian meal. Chutneys are blended fruits and vegetables, while pickles are cooked vegetable and fruit sauces. Chutneys are best served fresh (especially since many include uncooked ingredients), however they may be kept up to a week if refrigerated. Pickles — correctly bottled and sealed — can keep for long periods.

The amount of chillies you use controls the 'heat' of the chutney or pickle. If you are serving a hot chutney or pickle with your meal, it is best to balance it with others that are sweet, fruity, tangy or spicy.

Speciality shops stocking Indian food and accompaniments are a good source for commercial chutneys, pickles and sauces. It is often advisable to have some of these ready-made products on hand should you not have the time to make your own.

Aubergine Pickle

30 g green ginger
2 cloves garlic
600 mL vinegar
2 tablespoons chilli powder
2 teaspoons turmeric
2 teaspoons ginger powder
2 kg aubergines
125 g green chillies
300 mL sesame or groundnut oil
1 dessertspoon cumin seeds
1 dessertspoon fenugreek seeds
2 heaped tablespoons salt
250 g sugar

Scrape the ginger and cut into small pieces.
Slice the garlic finely and grind to a paste with a little of the vinegar and the chilli powder, turmeric and ginger powder.
Wash and dry the aubergines and the green chillies and cut into 2.5 cm pieces.
Heat oil till smoking. Cool and put in the cumin and fenugreek seeds and fry for a minute.
Add the paste and fry over a low flame till it smells cooked and the oil floats on top.
Add the rest of the vinegar, the salt and sugar and mix thoroughly. Add the aubergines, chillies and ginger and cook till the oil floats on top. Taste and if more salt is required add while hot. Cool and bottle.
Leave for a fortnight before using.

Green Pepper Pickle

500 g green peppers
500 g green tomatoes
8 onions
125 g salt
625 g brown sugar
900 mL vinegar
2 tablespoons clove powder
2 tablespoons cinnamon powder

Wash, dry and slice the green peppers and tomatoes.
Peel and slice the onions finely.
Sprinkle green peppers, tomatoes and onion slices with the salt.
Put a weight on them and let them stand all night.
Next morning drain off the moisture.
Put in saucepan, add the sugar and other ingredients.
Cover with the vinegar and simmer the mixture for 2 hours.
Let the mixture get quite cold.
Then bottle and keep for a week before using.

Hot Peach Pickle

1 kg nearly ripe peaches
500 g brown sugar
600 mL vinegar
250 g seedless sultanas
30 g chilli
1 teaspoon powdered ginger

Blanch the peaches in very hot water and remove the skins.
Split them open with a silver knife and extract the stones.
Boil the sugar in half the vinegar.
When the vinegar is boiling hot drop in the peach halves.
Simmer until they are quite soft, then add the sultanas, chilli and ginger and the remaining vinegar.
Reduce the liquid to desired thickness.
Remove from heat and stir well.
Let the mixture get quite cold.
Bottle and cork and eat after 15 days.

Mango Pickle

5 medium mangoes, peeled and minced
1 cup white sugar
½ cup white vinegar
5 mm slice ginger, pounded
2 teaspoons chilli powder
salt

Put minced mangoes in a saucepan and add sugar, vinegar, pounded ginger, chilli powder and salt to taste. Mix well, bring to the boil and simmer slowly for 10 minutes.
Reduce heat to low and continue to stir and cook

Aubergine Pickle

Green Pepper Pickle

until mangoes are soft and the mixture is jam-like in consistency.
Remove from heat, leave to cool, pour into a sterilised bottle, and seal.
Serve with rice, roast meat, curry or pooris.

Tomato Pickle

3 tomatoes, ripe or green, chopped or minced
4 fresh green chillies, chopped or minced
1 clove garlic crushed (optional)
½ teaspoon sugar
salt
thin slice of ginger, chopped or shredded finely
1 small onion, chopped or minced
3 tablespoons vinegar
pinch citric acid

Put tomatoes, chillies, garlic, sugar, salt to taste, ginger, onion and vinegar into a food processor and blend until mixture is smooth.
Alternatively, grind minced tomatoes, minced chillies, crushed garlic, sugar, salt, shredded ginger, minced onion and vinegar in mortar until mixture is as smooth as possible.
Remove mixture to a saucepan. Bring to the boil, reduce heat and simmer, stirring all the time, until mixture thickens.
Remove from heat, cool, and add citric acid. Stir well, pour into a sterilised botle, and seal.
Serve with Saffron Rice.

Mint Chutney (Poothena Chutney)

In a mortar pound a heaped teaspoonful of tamarind (free from stones and fibres) to a fine paste and then gradually pound into it a handful or more fresh mint leaves, 4 to 6 dry red chillies or fresh or pickled chillies and 2 cloves of garlic. Salt to taste. This chutney should be of the consistency of a paste. If necessary, moisten with a few drops of vinegar.

Coconut Chutney (Thainga Chutney)

½ of a finely scraped coconut or 2 heaped
   tablespoons of desiccated coconut

Sultana Chutney (p. 86)
Mint Chutney, Fresh Red Date Chutney (p. 86)
and Coriander Chutney

6 slices of fresh or pickled green ginger
3 or 4 dry red or fresh or pickled chillies
a clove or two of garlic
salt to taste

The above ingredients should be blended and pounded together into a paste with the addition of a little lemon juice.
Sometimes, the coconut used in making this chutney, instead of being scraped, is slightly roasted and then pounded.

Bengal Apple Chutney

60 g fresh ginger or 2 teaspoons ginger powder
1800 mL malt vinegar
125 g onions
60 g garlic
16 large cooking apples
500 g brown sugar
60 g mustard seed
1 tablespoon salt
15 g chilli powder
250 g raisins

Scrape ginger and wash in a little vinegar.
Mince the ginger, onions and garlic.
Peel and slice the apples.
Boil the apples and sugar in the vinegar till the apples are soft.
Add all the other ingredients and simmer for 15 to 20 minutes.
Use a wooden spoon while cooking and stir often.
Cool and bottle.

Coriander Chutney (Kothmir Chutney)

Pound a large handful of fresh coriander leaves to a paste with 4–6 green chillies, 4 thin slices green ginger and 2 cloves garlic. Add salt and lemon juice to taste.
Green coriander, like mustard and cress, is easily grown in shallow boxes either under glass or in the open in summer time. It is also readily available at specialty food shops and some greengrocers.
Chilli plants can also be grown under glass and will bear fruit but the chillies will not be as pungent as those in the East.

Fresh Red Date Chutney

3 dates
½ small onion
3 cloves garlic
¼ teaspoon chilli
½ teaspoon paprika
¼ teaspoon cumin
1 teaspoon salt
1 dessertspoon malt vinegar

Soak the dates, peel and chop the onion, peel the cloves of garlic.
Mince finely all the ingredients except the salt and vinegar, which should be mixed in well after mincing.
Serve.
This is eaten with vegetable fritters or pakoras as they are called in Northern India.

Mango Chutney

6 medium sized mangoes (green)
salt to taste
4 cloves garlic
30 g fresh ginger
6 large dry red chillies
600 mL malt vinegar
60 g almonds
375 g sugar
125 g raisins

Peel and slice the manoges and sprinkle with salt.
Grind the garlic, ginger and chillies to a paste with a little vinegar.
Blanch and chop the almonds.
Boil the vinegar and add sugar and mangoes and cook for 5 minutes over a low heat.
Add the garlic, ginger and chilli paste and cook for 10 minutes.
Add the almonds and raisins and cook for 5 minutes more.
Add salt to taste.
Cool and bottle.

Sultana Chutney

750 g seeded sultanas
60 g fresh ginger
60 g garlic cloves
30 g blanched almonds
450 mL malt vinegar
375 g moist brown sugar
60 g salt
10 g red dried chillies

Slice the sultanas thinly.
Peel the ginger and cut into thin slices.
Peel the garlic cloves and slice thinly.
Soak the sultanas in the vinegar for 24 hours.
Then mix all the ingredients in a saucepan, and bring to the boil.
Simmer uncovered until vinegar is the consistency of a syrup.
Remove from stove and allow to get quite cold.
Bottle and cork.
This can be eaten the next day.

Fresh Mint Chutney with Yoghurt

12 sprigs mint
1 onion
½ green capsicum
2 tablespoons desiccated coconut
2 tablespoons hot milk
10 tablespoons yoghurt
½ teaspoon salt

Wash the mint.
Peel and halve the onion.
Wash and dry the green capsicum.
Chop all three very fine.
Soak the coconut in the hot milk for 30 minutes.
Beat yoghurt till thin.
Add salt.
Mix all the ingredients well together.
Serve cold.
This is especially good with pilaus.

Spicy Sauce

1 tablespoon cooking oil
1 onion, chopped finely
2 cloves garlic, crushed
1 cup tomato sauce
½ teaspoon Worcestershire sauce
1 tablespoon chilli sauce (optional)
125 g canned pineapple pieces
1 tablespoon vinegar
2 teaspoons sugar

Heat oil in frying pan, add chopped onions and garlic and fry until lightly browned.
Reduce heat to low and add tomato sauce, Worcestershire sauce, chilli sauce (optional), and pineapple pieces. Mix well, bring to the boil, reduce heat and boil slowly, stirring for 5 minutes. Remove from heat and pour into a bowl.
This is good as a dip with meat balls or vegetables.
Serves 4-6.

Kebab Sauce

1 large onion, minced
thin slice ginger, pounded
5 stalks fresh mint, pounded
1 fresh green chilli, pounded
1 tablespoon fresh lemon juice
salt to taste

Mix all ingredients in a bowl, or place in a food processor and blend into a sauce.
Store in the refrigerator until needed.
Serve with Kebabs.
Serves 4-6.
Note: If a hotter sauce is required, increase the number of chillies to 3 or 4.

Chutneys, pickles, sambals and sauces

DESSERTS AND SWEETS

As in other countries, meals in India are usually rounded off with a dessert or a dish of sweets. Indian desserts often have a milk base to which cereals, vegetables and fruit are added. For sweetening, either sugar (refined or unrefined) or jaggery (brown sugar) is used.

There are hundreds of different varieties of sweets in India, and each region has its own specialities. Typical Bengali sweets are *rasgullas*, *rasmolai* and *gulab jamun* (milk sweets). In the North, *jalebi* (milk sweets) and *barfi* (a kind of milk-based fudge) are typical. Various kinds of *halvas*, prepared from vegetables, fruits, nuts and eggs are widely popular.

This chapter includes many delicious desserts and sweets which provide a balanced ending to any meal, particularly a spicy Indian one.

In the fruit dessert recipes, almost any combination of fresh or canned fruit may be tried.

As an alternative to a cooked dessert, consider some of the following ideas to round off your Indian meal: a platter of fresh fruit — grapes, slices of melon, strawberries, pineapple, mangoes, pawpaw and lychees, or any fruit in season; a selection of Indian sweets (available in speciality shops) with chocolate, and perhaps some almonds and muscatel grapes; natural or flavoured yoghurt, either served alone or with fresh or canned fruit; full cream ice-cream, plain or flavoured; a selection of nuts in the shell, with glace fruits and dried fruits such as figs, dates and apricots.

Firnee

60 g rice flour
600 mL milk
90 g sugar
1 teaspoon rose water or
1 green cardamom, coarsely ground
6 almonds
6 pistachio nuts

Mix the rice flour with a little cold milk and water. Bring the milk to the boil, remove from heat and mix in the flour paste.

Cook over gentle heat till it thickens slightly, then add sugar and allow to thicken further.

Flavour with the rose water and pour into a dish or into individual bowls.

Sprinkle with almonds (blanched and chopped) and pistachios.

Serve chilled.

Serves 4-6.

Firnee

89

Parsee Custard

900 mL milk
60 g castor sugar
5 eggs
1 tablespoon ground almonds
1 tablespoon rose water
pinch nutmeg and cardamom powder

Boil the milk and sugar together on a low heat till quantity is reduced to half.
Allow to cool a little and gradually add 3 whole eggs plus 2 egg yolks, well beaten together.
Add the almonds and rose water.
Pour the custard into a dish and sprinkle with nutmeg and cardamom powders.
Pre-heat the oven to 200°C (400°F).
Place dish in a pan of hot water, and bake for 45 minutes to 1 hour till the custard is set.
This sweet is eaten at Parsee weddings.
Serves 6-8.

Parsee Custard

Sweet Saffron Rice

This rich dessert is the Indian equivalent of English creamed rice.

30 g almonds
30 g raisins
½ teaspoon saffron strands
2 tablespoons hot milk
45 g ghee
250 g parboiled rice
¼ teaspoon salt
3 cardamoms
1 inch stick cinnamon
8 tablespoons cold milk
4 tablespoons sugar
2 tablespoons thick cream
30 g walnuts (shelled)

Blanch, slice and toast the almonds. Clean and fry the raisins. Toast the saffron strands, crumble them and

Sweet Saffron Rice

soak in the hot milk.
Heat the ghee. Add the rice, salt and spices and fry
for 3 minutes.
Add the cold milk and sugar and cook, covered, till
the rice is fully cooked. Now add the cream and
sprinkle with the saffron milk. Cover and cook for a
minute.
Remove to a hot serving dish, sprinkle with almond
slices, walnuts and raisins and serve.
Serves 6-8.

Semolina Pudding

15 g almonds
3 tablespoons melted butter
15 g currants
900 mL milk
7 tablespoons castor sugar
125 g semolina
1 teaspoon vanilla essence

½ teaspoon ground cardamom (optional)
½ teaspoon grated nutmeg (optional)

Blanch the almonds and slice thinly.
Heat the butter, fry the almonds to a very light cream
and remove from pan.
In the same fat fry the currants and set aside.
Divide the milk in half and put into two saucepans.
Add the sugar to one portion.
Bring both portions of milk to the boil, and simmer
on a very low heat.
In a third pan put all the melted butter and fry the
semolina very gently.
Stir constantly and do not let the semolina get creamy
coloured.
Now add the sugarless milk and keep stirring so that
no lumps are formed.
Add the sweetened milk gradually.
Add the vanilla essence and pour into a serving dish
while still of a fairly loose consistency.
When cold, sprinkle with the almonds, currants and
spice powder.
Serves 8-10.

Seviyan (Vermicelli Pudding)

A rich and filling dessert.

2 tablespoons ghee or butter
3 cardamom pods, crushed or pinch cardamom powder
170 g thin vermicelli
2 cups water
1 cup sugar
1 drop yellow food colouring (optional)
60 g almonds, chopped and fried lightly
125 g cashew nuts, fried lightly
30 g pistachio nuts, chopped (optional)
2 drops vanilla essence
4 cups milk or 2 cups evaporated milk mixed with 2 cups water

Heat ghee or butter in a saucepan over a low heat, add cardamom and fry for 2 seconds only.
Add vermicelli and fry until light brown in colour, stirring often.
Add water and sugar, boil for 10 minutes over moderate heat, then add yellow colouring (optional), fried almonds, fried cashew nuts, pistachio nuts (optional) and vanilla essence. Mix well.
Reduce heat to low, add milk or evaporated milk, stir, bring to the boil and remove from heat. Pour into a serving dish.
Serve hot or cold.
Serves 4-6.
Note: If desired, lightly fried raisins may be added with the nuts.

Lychees with Honeydew Melon

3 cups honeydew melon, scooped into balls
1 can lychees with syrup

Mix fruits and syrup together. Chill.
Serve plain or with ice-cream.
Serves 6-8.

Melon Dessert

1 can fruit salad with syrup
2 bananas, sliced or diced
1 cup watermelon, scooped into balls
1 cup rockmelon (canteloupe), scooped into balls

Semolina Pudding (p. 91)

Mix fruits and syrup together. Chill.
Serve plain or with ice-cream or whipped fresh cream.
Serves 4-6.
Note: These two melon desserts look most attractive served in a glass bowl.

Banana Fritters

1 cup plain flour
pinch salt
1 egg, beaten
1 small can evaporated milk
4 bananas
1 cup cooking oil
½ cup castor sugar

Sift flour and salt into a bowl. Make a well in the centre of the flour, and into this pour the beaten egg. Blend the egg with the flour a little at a time by stirring in gradually increasing circles from the centre. As mixture thickens, add milk gradually, while continuing to stir, to form a smooth batter.
Allow to stand for 30 minutes.
Split bananas in half lengthwise.
Heat oil in a frying pan over moderate heat.
Dip bananas in the batter and deep fry until golden brown.
Remove, drain well, and roll in castor sugar.
Serve with cream.
Serves 4.

Jalebi

250 g flour
water
1 dessertspoon yoghurt
oil for frying

Syrup:
500 g sugar
600 mL water
inner seeds of 3 cardamoms
a few sprigs of saffron or a pinch of turmeric

Make a batter with the flour and water (about the consistency of a thin pancake batter).
Cover and let stand for 24 hours. Stir in the yoghurt.
Place just sufficient oil in a frying pan to float the jalebis.
Fill a funnel with the mixture (place a finger over the hole). Swirl the batter in figure eights or double circles into the hot fat.
Cook on both sides till golden brown. Place into warm syrup for a few minutes. Drain on kitchen paper.

Banana Fritters (p. 93)

Syrup:
Combine all the ingredients and bring to the boil.
Allow to simmer over a low heat for 5-10 minutes
until a thick syrup is formed. Keep warm.
Serves 4-6.

Semolina Cookies

2 cups plain flour
¼ cup semolina
1 cup sugar
¼ teaspoon bicarbonate of soda
155 g ghee (or more if needed)

In a bowl, mix flour, semolina, sugar and bicarbonate
of soda.
Melt ghee and add a little at a time to the bowl,
kneading the mixture to a soft dough. Form into balls
the size of a large marble, flatten and place them on
baking sheets or trays, leaving 40 mm space between
them.
Preheat oven to 180°C (350°F) and bake the cookies
for 20 minutes. Cookies will not brown, but should
move freely on the tray when cooked. Remove from

oven and allow to cool on the trays. When cold,
store in air-tight bottles.
Yield: 40-44.

Pastry for Pooris (Puffs)

500 g sifted plain flour with a pinch of salt added
120 g ghee
cold water

Lightly rub the ghee into the flour and make into a
light, pliable dough by adding cold water. Knead until
the dough is smooth and velvety.
Roll out thinly and stamp out circular pieces in the
size required. In the centre of each piece place a
quantity of whatever filling you are using. Wet the
edge of the pastry all round, fold in half and press the
edges down.
To cook:
Fry in boiling ghee until they are a light golden colour
on both sides, being careful not to overcook them. If
preferred they can also be baked.
Makes 24.

Banana Filling

Mash ripe bananas with a fork and mix with half their bulk of finely desiccated coconut. Sweeten to taste and flavour with essence of rosewater.

Pineapple Filling

Pour away the syrup from a can of crushed pineapple. Add half its bulk of desiccated coconut. Sweeten to taste.

Coconut Filling

Blend together 250 g desiccated coconut moistened with milk, 6 cardamoms (inner seeds only), 60 g sultanas, 30 g ground almonds and 125 g of sugar. If you wish ¼ teaspoon cardamom powder can be used instead of the seeds.

Barfi

200 g Khoya
To make khoya bring to boil 1 litre of milk and allow to simmer, stirring frequently to prevent burning. The milk will finally thicken to a porridge-like consistency after about 40 minutes.
50 g sugar
½ teaspoon cardamom seeds
20 g pistachio nuts
20 g almonds

Mix prepared khoya with sugar in a heavy based pan and cook gently. Mix in the nuts and cardamom seeds and then transfer the mixture to a shallow, buttered dish. Pour in the contents and spread evenly. Allow to cool and cut into square or diamond shapes. Serves 6-8.

Coconut Pooris

INDEX

Printed in Singapore